TEST SCORES

AND

WHAT THEY MEAN

PRENTICE-HALL INTERNATIONAL, INC.
London · Tokyo · Sydney · Paris
PRENTICE-HALL OF CANADA, LTD.
PRENTICE-HALL DE MEXICO, S.A.

TEST SCORES

AND

WHAT THEY MEAN

Howard B. Lyman

UNIVERSITY OF CINCINNATI

PRENTICE-HALL, INC., ENGLEWOOD CLIFFS, N.J. 1963

©—1963 by PRENTICE-HALL, INC.
Englewood Cliffs, N.J.

L.C. Catalog Card Number: 63-7378

Printed in the United States of America
90377-C

THIS BOOK IS AFFECTIONATELY
DEDICATED TO

2

PREFACE

When, three years ago, I sent an outline of this book to several publishers who print original paperbacks in Psychology, all expressed an interest, for this would be the first book to deal primarily with the *meaning* of test scores; most textbooks in tests and measurements have surprisingly little to say about the various types of score. Furthermore, this book is intended to meet the needs of test users with limited training in testing—needs which have long been ignored.

Although it was written primarily for individuals who want to know more about test scores, this book should be useful as a text for a short interpretation-oriented Measurements course, for a refresher course in Testing, or for an in-service course on the Meaning of Test Results. It could be used, too, as a supplementary text for courses in Tests and Measurements, Introductory Psychology, Educational Psychology, Individual Differences, etc. It would also be useful for collateral reading in Counseling and Guidance courses.

Because of the tremendous numbers of standardized tests being used in such a wide variety of settings, it is inevitable that many people with little or no training in testing are responsible for using test results. Many school teachers, admissions directors, personnel workers, and others, for example, are in positions which require their having access to test results; but their professional backgrounds may include little or no training in measurement. Pediatricians, child psychiatrists, social workers, and many others often express interest in test results—even though lacking instruction in their interpretation. Personnel managers who have come up from the ranks rarely have had any test training. Neither have most university deans. With the assistance of this book, such people can learn a great deal about what test scores mean—to the ultimate advantage of those who have taken the tests.

I have written informally in an attempt to make this book interesting and understandable to any intelligent adult, however uninformed he may be concerning tests and testing. Wherever possible I have illustrated my points with real-life examples. The book should be most helpful to professional workers who have had no specialized training in testing, but it should prove to be a convenient reference even for those who have had such training.

No book, of course, can be a complete substitute for thorough training and experience. There is no expectation that this book will make anyone a test expert. There is more to the use of tests in counseling, for example, than is mentioned here. This book contains little about measurement theory or test selection. It devotes little space to the description of any specific tests; indeed, most of the illustrative examples deal with hypothetical tests. The test user must learn the meaning of actual test variables from test manuals and the like. I have little to say about personality and interest tests, for I believe that the users of such tests need more training than they can hope to receive from this book; inevitably, though, there is much here that can help in understanding such tests, and I have mentioned them in occasional examples.

Without a special study of test scores, anyone is likely to confuse *percentage-correct scores* with *percentile ranks, percentile ranks* with *standard scores, standard scores* with *normalized-standard scores, normalized standard scores* with *IQ's,* etc. Without a sound knowledge of what such scores (and others) are like, no one can hope to understand test results.

Test Scores—and What They Mean contains an original classification of types of score, showing their logical bases and their interrelationships. Everything else in this book can be found in other sources—often in many other sources. In no single other source, though, can a test user find even a description of more than a few of the many scores in common use.

Especially helpful to most readers should be the conversion table, permitting a test user to change from one type of score to another (assuming a normal distribution). A simple chapter on statistics is included for those who lack knowledge in that direction. The chapter on profiles should help the reader to a better understanding of *significant* differences in score. The chapter on types of score should be helpful to nearly everyone who uses test results. Many readers will find the *glossary* enlightening.

This book has not been easy to write, for I have tried to keep in mind the reader who is greatly uninformed about tests. Most parts of the manuscript were given an additional polishing after being read to undergraduate students. For more than twenty years, I have been studying about or working with tests. I have borrowed freely from that experience to provide realistic and meaningful illustrative examples.

I want to acknowledge with thanks the instruction in testing and the encouragement to work with tests that I received from my own teachers—notably such men as Herbert Sorenson and Richard North (at the University of Kentucky); Donald G. Paterson, W. S. Miller, Howard P. Longstaff, Walter Cook, John G. Darley, and Ralph F. Berdie (at the University of Minnesota); and J. McVicker Hunt and Donald Lindsley (at Brown University). I want to acknowledge, too, the assistance of my typist, Frances Stivender, whose aid and encouragement were given most freely. Thanks are due also to Goldine Gleser for a critical reading of the chapter on statistics and for various suggestions. Others whose assistance in reading is most appreciated include Patricia Jackson and Zoe Lyman; their ability to detect errors, their willingness to suggest editorial changes, and their gracious interest were most helpful.

A final word of thanks is given to Dr. Robert Ebel, Educational Testing Service, Princeton, N.J., who read the entire manuscript and suggested a number of valuable changes.

HOWARD B. LYMAN

CONTENTS

CHAPTER THREE • BASIC ATTRIBUTES OF THE TEST (*Cont.*):

CHAPTER FOUR • A FEW STATISTICS   39

Chapter One # SCORE INTERPRETATION

"When am I going to start failing?" a student asked me a couple of years ago. Upon being questioned, he told me this story: "My high school teacher told me that my IQ is only 88. He said that I might be able to get into college because of my football, but that I'd be certain to flunk out—with an IQ like that!" I pointed out to Don that he had been doing well in my course. I found out that he had a B+ average for the three semesters he had completed. I reminded him that the proof of a pudding lies in its eating—and that the proof of scholastic achievement lies in grades, not in a test designed to predict grades.

Last June, Don graduated with honors.

This little story, true in all essential details, illustrates many points; for example:

1. Was the test score correct? I suspect that an error was made in administering or scoring the test. Or, perhaps that score was a *percentile rank* instead of an *IQ*—which would make a lot of difference.

2. Regardless of the accuracy of the score, the teacher should not have told him the specific value of his IQ on the test.

3. The teacher went far beyond proper limits in telling Don that he would ". . . be certain to flunk out. . . ." The teacher should have known that test scores are not perfect.

4. Furthermore, test scores do not determine future performance;

1

demonstrated achievement is more conclusive evidence than is a score on a test intended to predict achievement. Both the teacher and Don should have known that!

If Don's case were unusual, I might have forgotten about it; however, mistakes in interpreting tests occur every day. Here are three other examples that come quickly to mind:

> A college freshman, told that she had "average ability," withdrew from college. Her counselor had not added ". . . when compared with other college students." She reasoned that if she had only average ability compared with people in general, she must be very low when compared with college students; rather than face this, she dropped out of college. (There may have been other reasons, too, but this seemed to be the principal one.)

> A high school student who had high measured clerical and literary *interests* was told that this proved that he should become either a clerk or a writer!

> A personnel manager, learning that one of his best workers had scored very low on a test that eventually would be used in selecting future employees, nearly discharged the worker; ". . . the tests really opened our eyes about her. Why, she's worked here for several years, does good work, gets along well with the others. That test shows how she had us fooled!"

None of these illustrative cases is fictitious. All involve real people. And we will see a good many more examples of test interpretation throughout this book. Each one is based on a true situation, most of them drawn from my own experience in working with people who use tests.

No amount of anecdotal material, though, can show the thousands of instances every year in which the wrong persons are selected for jobs, admitted to schools and colleges, granted scholarships, and the like—merely because someone in authority is unable to interpret available test scores or, equally bad, places undue confidence in the results.

Nor will anecdotal material reveal the full scope of the misinformation being given to students and parents by teachers and others who are trying to help. Willingness to help is only the first step. There is also a lot to know about the meaning of test scores. Even the expert who works daily with tests has to keep his wits with him, for this is no game for dullards.

Testing Today

What is testing like today?

The quality of tests has improved over the past two or three decades. Most test authors and test publishers are competent and service-motivated; they subscribe to ethical standards that are commendably high. Each year universities turn out greater numbers of well-trained measurements people. More and more teachers and personnel workers are being taught the fundamentals of testing. In spite of these and other positive influences, we still find a desperate need for wider understanding of what test scores mean.

About one million tests per school day are being used in American schools alone! Add to this number the tests that are being given in industry, personnel offices, employment bureaus, hospitals, civil service agencies, etc.—add all of these in, and we can conclude that there is a great deal of testing being done.

Who will interpret the test scores? Often, nobody will. In literally millions of instances, the test scores never progress beyond the point of being recorded on a file card or folder; indeed, this seems to be the official policy of many personnel offices and school systems. In other instances, the scores are made available to supervisors or teachers; these people may, at their discretion, interpret the results.

These people should receive the test results and make use of them. They also should interpret the scores to the examinees. Unfortunately many people with legitimate access to test results have had no training in measurement, and certainly little or no training in how to interpret test scores. I should not have been surprised by this incident:

> I was asking about some test scores made by Dick Davis, a boy in whom I had a particular interest. As an eighth-grader in a large school system, he was being used in a research study and had taken an extensive test battery. The homeroom teacher, Pamela Pretti, must have been taught that tests should be kept secure; she extracted a key from her handbag, unlocked her desk, took out a ring of keys, selected one, and unlocked a storage closet; from the closet, she drew a folder out from underneath a stack of books. Miss Pretti promptly read off a long list of scores made by young Dick. "What tests are these?" I asked. She didn't know. "Do these scores compare Dick with the national norm group, the local school norm group, or

with just those in the research project?" She didn't know. Nor could she tell me anything about tests that Dick had taken previously. She thought the counselor might have that information—or perhaps it was the principal's office—she wasn't sure.

Now, I've known Miss Pretti for years. I know that she is a good teacher, and I know that her students like her. But she was taught very little in college about the use of tests, and her work today keeps her busy. Consequently she finds it easy to pay no attention to the standardized tests taken by her students. She reasons that Lester Lathrop, the counselor, knows more about tests and will take care of any test interpretation that needs to be done.

Mr. Lathrop is a certified school counselor and a good one. In tests and measurements, he has had only a little training because he had to take courses for a teaching certificate before he could start his counselor preparation. He wants to take more courses in measurement, but it is difficult now that he has family responsibilities. He tries to see his students as often as he can, but he has nearly 1,000 students to counsel.

As you have suspected, many students are never told their test results. Who has time?

This school system is a good one. Its policies are enlightened, and its personnel are interested in their students. Testing is not, after all, the school's most important activity. Good tests are selected, administered, scored, and recorded properly; and some teachers do a remarkable job of using the test results and in interpreting the results to their students.

The typical school system has few teachers who are well trained in testing, because most teachers have had little opportunity to take elective courses while in college. Only a very few states require even a single course in tests and measurements.

Even those teachers who have had a course have probably learned less about the meaning of test scores than they have about the qualities of a good test, the principles of measurement, and the construction of classroom tests.

Personnel workers in industry often have no training in tests and measurement. Test interpretation in industry is even worse than in education—except for one thing: industry seldom gives tests for purposes of individual guidance.

Many people whose positions demand that they have access to test results have had no real training in what test scores mean. I hope that this book will help people with limited backgrounds in testing to attain a better understanding of test scores and test interpretation.

Institutional and Individual Decisions

Tests are often used as tools in reaching decisions. Some decisions are *institutional;* that is, the decisions are made in behalf of an institution (school, college, corporation, etc.) and such decisions are made frequently. Two examples of such institutional decisions are: which persons to select and which to reject, and where to place a particular examinee. Often tests can be extremely effective in such situations because they help the institution to reach a higher percentage of good decisions. And an occasional bad decision about an individual examinee is not likely to have any adverse effect on the institution. Tests can be used more effectively to predict the performance of a group than they can to predict the performance of an individual.

> Let us test a random sample of 1,000 fifth-grade pupils. Let me have the top fifty pupils, and you take the bottom fifty pupils. You may decide what these one hundred pupils are to be taught. You may have a team of experts to help you teach your pupils; I will teach mine myself. At the end of one semester, we will give both groups the same final examination. Regardless of the subject matter taught, I am sure that my group will be higher on the average. On the other hand, it is probable that some of your pupils will outscore some of mine—despite that tremendous original difference in ability. Which of your pupils will show this tremendous response to superior teaching? Which of my pupils will lag far behind the others? I doubt whether we can predict very accurately which ones these would be; however, we can have considerable confidence in predicting that my group will have the higher average achievement.

A second general type of decision is the individual decision. Here, the individual must make a decision which will affect himself or, perhaps, a son or daughter. The individual has no backlog of similar decisions, and he may never have to reach a comparable decision again. The situation is unique insofar as the individual is concerned, and a wrong decision may have a lasting effect on him. Typical examples of individual decisions include: whether to accept a certain job offer, whether to go to college, which college to attend, which curriculum to study, which course to take, or which girl to marry. Tests sometimes help, but they are rarely so helpful as in institutional decisions; and they are always far less accurate in individual situations.

Two Meanings of Interpretation

These decision types, introduced by Cronbach and Gleser, suggest two distinct meanings for *test interpretation*. According to the first meaning, we need to understand test scores well enough to use them in making an institutional type of decision. The emphasis is on our personal understanding of the scores. Less skill is required for interpretation in this sense than when we must interpret the meaning of test scores to someone else. In this second meaning, test interpretation requires a thorough understanding of test scores plus an ability to communicate the results.

For the most part, I will make no effort to differentiate between these two meanings of interpretation; however, Chapter Nine is concerned almost entirely with the problem of telling other people what scores mean.

A PRETEST

As a pretest of your own ability to interpret test scores, try the following questions—typical of those asked by test-naïve teachers and personnel workers. If you answer the questions satisfactorily (answers at the end of this chapter), you will probably learn little from this book. If you cannot understand the questions, you certainly need this book! Let us see how you do.

1. Why can't we use the raw score itself in test interpretation?
2. What is the difference between a percentile rank and a percentage-correct score?
3. Why are norms important?
4. How constant is the IQ?
5. What is the difference between reliability and validity?
6. Is there any difference between a standard score and a normalized standard score?
7. What effect, if any, does the range of scores have on test reliability and validity?
8. Why, from a measurement point of view, should cheating be held to a minimum?

9. What statistic states the size of difference in scores on an individual's profile that is necessary for "significance"?
10. How can test difficulty influence the apparent performance or improvement of a school class?

Did you take the pretest? If not, go back and take it now—before reading the answers which follow.

ANSWERS TO PRETEST QUESTIONS

1. Why can't we use the raw score itself in test interpretation?

The raw score, based usually on the number of items answered correctly, depends so much on the number and difficulty of the test items that it is nearly valueless in test interpretation; however, because it provides the basis for all other types of scores, the raw score needs to be accurate. In other words, the raw score is basic—nothing can be more accurate than it is.

2. What is the difference between a percentile rank and a percentage-correct score?

A person's *percentile rank* describes his relative standing within a particular group: a percentile rank of 80 (P_{80}) means that a person's score was equal to or higher than the scores made by 80 per cent of the people in a specified group. A *percentage-correct score*, on the other hand, tells us nothing about a person's relative performance. It tells us only the percentage of items answered correctly; for example, a percentage correct score of 80 means that a person has answered 80 per cent of the test items correctly. Confusion between these two basically different types of score sometimes results in considerable embarrassment.

3. Why are norms important?

Norms give meaning to our scores. They provide a basis for comparing one individual's score with the scores of others who have taken the test. Ideally the test publisher describes the norm group or groups as precisely as possible, so that the user may decide how appropriate they are for reporting the performance of individuals in whom he is interested. Local norms, developed by the user, may be more appropriate in some situations than any of the publisher's norms. Norms tables are used to translate raw scores into derived scores such as percentiles, standard scores, grade-equivalent scores, intelligence quotients, and the like.

4. How constant is the IQ?

Volumes could be written (and have been) on this topic. Even under ideal conditions (for example, a short time between testings on the same test for a highly motivated young adult), we would expect to find slight differences in IQ from testing to testing. In general, changes in IQ tend to be greatest: among young children; when a long time separates the first and subsequent testings; when different tests are used; and when there is a marked difference in motivational level of the examinee at the different test sessions. Changes of five IQ points are common even under good conditions.

On the other hand, most people change relatively little in IQ. Only rarely will individuals vary so much as to be classified as normal or average at one time and either mentally retarded or near-genius at some other time.

The IQ is only a type of test score. Any fluctuation or inaccuracy in test performance will be reflected in the scores and will help to cause differences in score.

5. What is the difference between reliability and validity?

Reliability refers to the consistency of measured performance. *Validity* refers to a test's ability to measure what we want it to. High reliability is necessary for reasonable validity, because a test that does not measure consistently cannot measure anything well; however, a test may be highly reliable without being able to do any specified task well.

6. Is there any difference between a standard score and a normalized standard score?

Yes, a big difference. A *standard score* is a method of stating how much (in standard-deviation units) a given score differs from the arithmetic mean; thus, $z = (X - \overline{X})/s$, where: $X =$ raw score; $\overline{X} =$ arithmetic mean; and $s =$ standard deviation. There are several modifications of this z-score, in all of which the shape of distribution remains the same as that which we had in the distribution of raw scores; therefore, we can convert from raw to standard scores without altering in any way the shape of the distribution of original values. If desired, we could also convert the standard scores back to the raw scores. Thus, standard scores are linear transformations of raw scores.

With normalized standard scores, though, we do modify the shape of the distribution of raw scores. In effect, the test publisher converts the raw scores to percentiles—then assigns the standard score values that these percentiles would have in a normal distribution. We cannot convert normalized standard score values back to the original raw scores, for the precise score identification has been lost. Normalized standard scores are area, not linear, transformations of raw scores.

7. What effect does the range of scores have on test reliability and validity?

Variability has a great effect on both reliability and validity. Other things being equal, a greater range in scores makes for higher reliability and validity coefficients. The sophisticated test user bears this fact in mind when he reads reliability and validity coefficients in test manuals.

8. Why, from a measurement point of view, should cheating be held to a minimum?

In addition to the obvious moral and ethical considerations that might be mentioned, cheating reduces the validity of a test. The amount of help a person will get by cheating on a given test varies. This amount of help, a *variable error*, tends to reduce the reliability of the test. Because validity depends on reliability (*see* Question 5 above), the lowered reliability may result in reduced validity. Therefore, test users who want valid results will discourage cheating.

9. What statistic states the size of difference in scores on an individual's profile that is necessary for "significance"?

This is a trick question. As we will see in subsequent chapters, there are statistics which give us some idea as to how far apart a person's scores must be before we can be reasonably sure that they are truly different; however, no single statistic answers the question directly and satisfactorily.

10. How can test difficulty influence the apparent performance or improvement of a school class?

If a test is far too easy for a class, the pupils will obtain scores that are lower than they should be; we cannot tell how much better the pupils might have been able to do if there had been more items of suitable difficulty. If they are given a test of appropriate difficulty some time later, the pupils will appear to have made greater gains than we should expect; now they are not prohibited (by the very content of the test) from attempting items of reasonable difficulty, and there are fewer students with near-perfect scores.

There are many other facets to the problem of item difficulty. Some of these will be considered later in this book.

How did you do?

Chapter Two

TYPES

OF TEST

Can we be interested in something without being any good at it? Of course! And yet:

> A school counselor is reporting *interest* test results to a high school junior and his father: "John scored high on Computational and Mechanical. This means that he should go on to college and study Mechanical Engineering."

Maybe John will become a good mechanical engineer. Maybe not. No interest test will tell us. What about his intelligence? His aptitudes? His grades in school? His ability to pay for college training? Many factors besides interest-test scores are involved in deciding whether anyone should go to college or in the choosing of a vocational objective.

Interest and aptitude are not synonymous, but they are often confused by test users. And there are so many terms used in describing different types of test that it is easy to become confused. In this chapter I will present several classification systems and define a number of assorted terms.

MAXIMUM-PERFORMANCE vs. TYPICAL-PERFORMANCE TESTS

All tests may be classified as measuring either *maximum* or *typical performance*. Tests of maximum performance ask the examinee to do his best work; his ability, either attained or potential, is being tested. With tests of typical performance, we hope to obtain some ideas as to what the examinee is really like or what he actually does—rather than what he is capable of doing.

Maximum-Performance Tests

Included under maximum-performance tests are tests of intelligence, aptitude, and achievement. In all of these, we assume that the examinees are equally and highly motivated. To the extent that this assumption is not justified, we must discount the results. Since we rarely know how well persons were motivated while taking a test, we usually must accept the assumption or have the person retested.

> Private Peter Panner was in the army for several years before the start of World War II. During that time, he took so many tests (many of them experimental or research editions) that he paid little attention to them. Not infrequently he would loaf through a test, making no effort to obtain a good score. As World War II approached, he wanted to attend Officer Candidate School; he found that the army required a score of at least 110 on the *Army General Classification Test,* and that his score had been only 92. Peter was given permission to retake the test and scored well above the cutoff score of 110.

At least three determinants are involved in every score on a test of maximum performance: innate ability, acquired ability, and motivation. There is no way to determine how much of a person's score is caused by any one of these three determinants—they are necessarily involved in every maximum-performance score; that is, a person's test score necessarily depends in part on his inborn potential as it has been modified by his life experiences (his education and training, his environment, etc.), and by his motivation at the time of testing.

Intelligence Tests

Intelligence is an abstract concept. We all have ideas about its meaning, but there is little general agreement as to its precise meaning. Just as you may have your own definition and I may have my own, so, too, does the author of each intelligence test have his own.

Intelligence tests reflect these differences in definition. Some include only verbal items; others contain much nonverbal material. Some stress problem-solving while others emphasize memory. Some intelligence tests result in a single total score (perhaps an IQ), whereas others yield several scores.

These varying emphases lead to diverse results. We should expect to find different IQ's when the same person is tested with different tests. We may be obtaining several measures of intelligence, but each time intelligence is being defined just a little differently. Under the circumstances, perhaps we should be surprised whenever different intelligence tests give us nearly the same results.

Intelligence has many pseudonyms: mental maturity, general classification, scholastic aptitude, general ability, mental ability, college ability, primary mental abilities, etc. They all mean about the same as intelligence although they may differ somewhat in emphasis or application.

For most purposes, intelligence tests may be thought of as tests of general aptitude or scholastic aptitude. When so regarded, they are most typically used in predicting achievement in school, college, or training programs.

Aptitude Tests

All aptitude tests imply prediction. They give us a basis for predicting future level of performance. Aptitude tests often are used in selecting individuals for jobs, for admission to training programs, for scholarships, etc. Sometimes aptitude tests are used for classifying individuals—as when college students are assigned to different ability-grouped sections of the same course.

Achievement Tests

Achievement tests are used in measuring present level of knowledge, skills, competence, etc. Unlike other types of test, many achievement tests are produced locally. A teacher's classroom test is a good example. There are also many commercially developed achievement tests.

DIFFERENTIATING TYPES OF MAXIMUM-PERFORMANCE TESTS

The principal basis for differentiating between aptitude and achievement tests lies in their use. The same test may be used, in different situations, to measure aptitude and achievement. The purpose of the testing, whether for assessing present attainment or for predicting future level of performance, is the best basis for distinction.

As noted above, intelligence tests are often regarded as aptitude tests. Some intelligence tests could give us a fair indication of academic achievement—though they are rarely (if ever) used in this manner. And achievement tests obviously measure intelligence to some extent.

With tests of maximum performance, we seldom have difficulty in understanding what we are measuring for. With aptitude tests, we are trying to predict how well people will do. With achievement tests, we are trying to measure their present attainment. With intelligence tests, though we may disagree on specific definitions, we are trying to measure level of intellectual capacity or functioning.

Typical-Performance Tests

The situation is far less clear with tests of typical performance. There is less agreement about what is being measured or what should be measured. To start with, there is a tremendous proliferation of terms: adjustment, personality, temperament, interests, preferences, values, etc. There are tests, scales, blanks, inventories, indexes, etc. And there are Q-sorts, forced-choice methods, etc.—to say nothing about projective techniques, situational tests, and the like.

What does a score mean? It is very hard to say—even after having given the matter careful thought. In the first place, the scales of a typical-performance test are likely to be vaguely defined: what is sociable to one author may not be to the next. Then, too, the philosophy or rationale underlying typical-performance tests must necessarily be more involved and less obvious than the rationale for an aptitude or achievement test.

Whereas a person's ability is more or less stable, his affective nature is likely to change over a short period of time. And it is this aspect of the individual that we try to get at through tests of typical performance. We are trying to find out what a person is really like, how he typically reacts or feels.

With maximum-performance tests, we are certain at least that a person did not obtain a higher score than he is capable of; after all, one can't fake knowing more algebra or fake being more intelligent. With typical-performance tests, though, a person usually can fake in either direction (higher or lower, better adjustment or poorer adjustment, etc.). With these tests, we do not want the examinee to do the best he can; instead, we want him to answer as honestly as he can.

There would seem to be an assumption that an examinee was trying to answer honestly. On some personality tests, though, the authors have been concerned only with the response made, rather than with the examinee's reasons for having made it. Thus, the person who responds *Yes* to an item may do so honestly, or he may be trying to look better or to look worse than he really is; it makes no difference, for he resembles specified other people at least to the extent that he, too, made the same response.

Criterion-Keying

Some typical-performance tests are said to be *criterion-keyed*, because their scoring keys have been developed through the performance of two contrasting groups, as:

> We decide to construct a *Progressivism and Liberalism Index* (*PALI*). After defining what we mean by progressivism and liberalism, we decide that an ultraconservative group—say, the James Burke Society (JBS)—should obtain very low scores if our test is valid; we decide, too, that members of the American Association for Civil Liberties (AACL) should obtain high scores. We write a large number of items that seem relevant and administer them to members of both groups. With the aid of statistics, we retain for our *PALI* those items which discriminate best between the JBS and the AACL, regardless of whether the result seems logical. We might, for example, find more members of JBS than members of AACL answering *Yes* to: *Do you consider yourself a liberal individual?* Regardless of the real-life accuracy or inaccuracy of the responses,

we still might retain this item—counting a response of *No* as one score point in the liberal direction.

Typical-performance tests which are criterion-keyed often seem superior to tests for which the scoring keys have been developed in other ways. Criterion-keyed tests sometimes are criticized because occasional items are scored in a way that seems to make little sense; the answer to this criticism is of course that the scoring system "works."

Forced-Choice Items

Forced-choice is a term being heard with increasing frequency. An item is *forced-choice* if the alternatives have been matched for social acceptability, even though only one alternative relates to a particular criterion. The simplest form of forced-choice item has two alternatives, each seeming to be equally desirable:

> *Would you rather be: (a) honest; (b) loyal?*

I would like to be both—and you would, too. Perhaps, though, some group (say, good bookkeepers) could be found statistically to answer (*a*) more often than less good bookkeepers. Forced-choice items may have the advantage of being somewhat disguised as to intent, but they are not unanimously favored. They may be resented by examinees because of the fine discriminations demanded.

Ambiguity of Items

With nearly all typical-performance test items, there is likely to be some ambiguity. Let us take the item:

> *I am a liberal.*
> *Strongly Agree   Agree   Don't Know   Disagree   Strongly Disagree*

If I had to answer this item, my reasoning might go something like this:

What do they mean by *liberal?* I could say *Strongly Agree,* for I am strongly opposed to censorship. My political views are largely conservative, so I could answer *Disagree;* in fact, I am sure that some of my colleagues think that I ought to answer *Strongly Disagree*—considering my views on the _____ Bill. In honesty, I should not say that I *Don't Know.* But the truth is that I am sometimes liberal and sometimes not!

The indecisiveness of an examinee may be caused by the ambiguity of a term, or it may be a reflection of the individual's personality. In either case, the examinee may answer an item sometimes one way and sometimes another, and be perfectly sincere each time. (As we shall see in Chapter Three, such factors as these lower test reliability.)

Use Caution! There are other reasons, too, why typical-performance tests should be viewed with caution. The very nature of these tests is such that individualized meanings of the items become important. Let us take the item:

I am a liberal.   True   False

This may be answered *True* by many conservatives who believe that they are more liberal than their friends; and some liberals, feeling that they are less liberal in their views than they would like to be, may answer the item, *False.* (Note, however, that this would make no difference if the test were criterion-keyed.)

Furthermore, the motivational pattern of each examinee becomes of great importance. With maximum-performance tests, we want each examinee to do his best. The case is not so simple though with typical-performance tests. If the examinee has much to gain by showing up well, he may try to answer the items so that he will appear to be better than he really is. Similarly, he may try to appear more disturbed than he really is if that would be to his advantage. And he may do so either deliberately or subconsciously.

Still further, most typical-performance tests try to measure several different characteristics of the individual. A person who fakes, deliberately or not, along one scale of the test may inadvertently change his scores on other measured characteristics as well. For example, the person who tries to appear more *sociable* may inadvertently score higher on the *aggressive* scale, too.

Test norms are based on groups of people (perhaps students) in nonthreatening situations. To compare the performance of a person under stress (of being selected for a job, of severe personal problems, or whatever) with the performance of such groups is rather unrealistic.

Typical-performance tests, of course, can be useful to skilled counselors; however, they rarely should be interpreted by people who have only limited backgrounds in testing and psychology. There are so many pitfalls to be aware of. The tests do have their place—but that place is not in the hands of the amateur.

For all of these reasons—and more—most psychologists feel that we can place much less confidence in typical-performance tests than in the maximum-performance tests with which we shall be principally concerned.

Objective—Subjective—Projective

Another way of looking at tests gives us a classification according to the form of response called for. One familiar classification is *objective* vs. *essay*. This classification is probably better stated as *objective* vs. *subjective*, and I would add *projective*. A little later I will mention a similar classification, one that I prefer even though it is less common.

An item is objective if the complete scoring procedure is prescribed in advance of the scoring. Thus, multiple-choice and true-false tests are usually objective, for the test-writer can draw up a scoring key which contains the right (or best) answer for each item on the test. Except for mistakes or for difficulties in reading responses, we can be completely objective. When answered on special answer sheets, such items can even be scored by machine.

I dislike using *essay* as opposed to *objective*. An essay item is a specific type of item (asking the examinee to write an essay of greater or lesser length on an assigned topic); it is not broad enough to be considered a general type. *Subjective* is better, for it is more inclusive and indicates that some element of personal judgment will be involved in the scoring. Completion items are another example of subjective items, for the tester usually cannot anticipate every possible answer that may be scored as correct.

Projective items are, in a sense, subjective items—but they are something more. They are items which are deliberately made ambiguous to permit individualistic responses. The Rorschach inkblots, Allen's *Three-Dimensional Personality Test*, Murray's *Thematic Apperception Test* are examples. Verbal material may be used projectively, too; Rotter, for example, presents the examinee

with stems of sentences to be completed, thereby making him
project his personality into the response. Typical of Rotter's items
are:

> *I like to . . .*
> *One thing I dread is . . .*
> *My mother . . .*

Select-Response—Supply-Response

A similar classification scheme, one which I prefer, is *select-
response* vs. *supply-response.* If the examinee must select his response from among the alternatives which are presented to him,
the test-writer can specify the scoring key completely and the items
will be objective. Although complete objectivity is not possible
with most materials when the examinee must supply the response
himself, near-complete objectivity can be obtained with some
material.

I have tried to stress objectivity of scoring. Any time we prepare
a test, whether for classroom use or for national distribution, we
must decide what items to write, what elements of information to
include, what wording to use, etc. Inevitably there is some degree
of subjectivity in test-making.

Written—Oral

Another basis for test classification is found in the medium used
for presenting the directions and the item material. Most typically,
test items are printed or written and the examinee responds by
writing his answers or by making marks which correspond to chosen
answers. Directions sometimes are given orally, but most frequently
are given both orally and in writing.

Rather few tests are oral. Teacher-prepared spelling tests are the
principal example. A few tests are available on sound recordings.
There are tests for blind people, some of which were especially developed for them and others which are simply adaptations of tests
for the sighted. And there are trade tests, prepared for oral presentation and oral response, used almost exclusively in employment
offices.

Standardized—Informal

Standardized tests are tests which have been developed, usually by specialists, for more extensive use than by the test-writer himself. The test content is set, the directions prescribed, the scoring procedure more or less completely specified. In addition, there are almost always norms against which we may compare the scores of our examinees.

Informal tests, on the other hand, refer primarily to tests which have been written by the examiner for his own use. We are not concerned with such tests in this book; however, much that is said about standardized tests will have some application to informal tests, too.

Speed—Power

Speeded tests are tests in which speed plays an important part in determining a person's score; however, a test may have a time limit and still not be speeded. If there is no time limit or if the time limit is so generous that most examinees are able to finish, the test is said to be a *power test.*

Most achievement tests should be power tests, for we are likely to be more concerned with assessing our examinees' levels of attainment than we are in finding out how rapidly they respond. Even here, though, there are exceptions: for example, an achievement test in shorthand or typing. We cannot say categorically whether speed or power is more important in aptitude and intelligence tests, for each has its place.

We have used power and speed as if they were separate categories. It would be more accurate to think of them as opposite ends of a continuum. Some tests are almost purely power (having no time limit), and other tests are almost purely speed (having items of such little difficulty that everyone could answer them perfectly if given enough time); in between these extremes, though, are many tests with time limits, some generous and some limited. Such in-between tests have some characteristics of both speed and power tests and are best classified as being one or the other, depending upon whether the time limit makes speed an important determinant of score.

Group—Individual

This classification is perhaps most obvious of all. An *individual* test is one which can be administered to only one individual at a time. Common examples are individual tests of intelligence, such as the *Stanford-Binet* and the *Wechsler* tests. Some tests that involve special apparatus, such as manual dexterity tests, usually are administered individually; however, such tests can be administered simultaneously to small groups if proper conditions exist and if the examiner has multiple copies available.

Group tests can be administered to more than one individual at a time and usually can be administered simultaneously to any size group. Group tests are usually *paper-and-pencil* (the only materials involved), but not necessarily so. Individual tests frequently, but not always, involve materials other than paper and pencil.

Paper-and-Pencil—Apparatus (*Performance*)

When special equipment is needed, the test may be called an *apparatus* test or, sometimes, a *performance* test. I don't like this use of *performance,* for the term is already overworked—being a generic term for tested behavior (as . . . his performance on the test . . .), as well as a term that is sometimes used in opposition to verbal (as on the *Wechsler* tests, which yield Verbal and Performance IQ's).

Verbal—Nonverbal

A *verbal test* has verbal items; that is, the items involve words (either oral or written). So-called *nonverbal* tests contain no verbal items; however, words almost always are used in the directions. Some writers prefer to use nonlanguage for tests which have no verbal items but for which the directions are given either orally or in writing; these writers would use nonverbal only for tests where no words are used, even in the directions.

Machine-Scored—Hand-Scored

Until very recently, *machine-scored* tests meant tests taken on special IBM answer sheets and scored on an IBM Test Scoring

Machine. Now, however, there are several types of scoring machine. The most common operate on one or more of three principles: (1) mark-sensing; (2) punched-hole; or (3) visual-scanning.

In mark-sensing, the scoring machine makes an electrical contact with a mark made with an exceptionally soft lead pencil. This is the basis for the IBM Test Scoring Machine. It is also the basis for another IBM scoring system where special pencil marks are made on IBM cards. A special machine reads these marks and punches holes corresponding to them; these cards can then be scored either with special equipment or with standard IBM accounting or statistical machines.

In punched-hole scoring, the responses may have been made either with mark-sensing pencils, or with special individual card punchers. The test cards are then scored either with special equipment or with standard IBM machines.

Electronic scoring is the latest development; here the process involves visual-scanning with an electric eye. Special pencils need not be used. Depending upon its complexity, the machine may be capable of scoring several different test parts simultaneously, of printing the scores on the answer sheets, of reading examinees' names off the answer sheets and preparing a roster, etc.

These are the principal types of scoring, but not the only ones. There are many other scoring machines; for example, one which literally weighs the number of correct responses with tiny weights on the pan of a scale, another which records correct responses whenever a puff of air is allowed to penetrate a special roll of paper through a player-piano-like hole, etc. Then, too, many teaching machines use programs which are only progressively difficult test items.

With very few exceptions, machine-scored tests could be *hand-scored*. Hand-scoring, though slower and more old fashioned, has some advantages—especially when nonstandardized tests are involved.

We need to use care in scoring tests, regardless of the method of scoring involved. Mistakes can be made under any system, and we cannot permit ourselves to be careless.

> I once contracted with a professional scoring service to machine-score several hundred interest tests. I noted that the service provided no check or verification of its results, so I hand-scored a small

sample of the tests. Every one of these hand-scored answer sheets revealed scoring errors on three different interest areas. After correspondence with the director of the scoring service, I learned that his service had been using faulty scoring keys on this test for several years.

Culture-Fair

Some tests are said to be *culture-fair* or *culture-free*. The latter term should be avoided, for no test can be developed completely free from cultural influences. Some tests, though, are relatively independent of cultural or environmental influences and may be thought of as being fair to people of most cultures; however, these tests may do less well than others in measuring individuals within our own culture. By using items that are relatively culture-free, such tests may not measure anything very effectively within any given culture.

How to Tell

How can we tell what a test is like? We can learn something about available tests by reading the catalogs of the various test publishers. This is not necessarily safe, though, for:

> A few years ago one test publisher listed an interest test under Aptitude in his catalog, "because," he told me privately, "it's the only interest test I have, and I didn't want to create a separate section for just one test."

This is admittedly an extreme example; however, test catalogs are created for the purpose of selling tests and are not the most objective source of information.

Nor are test titles the best means for telling what a test is. In the past, there have been many examples of tests with misleading titles; however, test publishers today are beginning to do a much better job of giving descriptive titles to their tests.

Test manuals are usually the best guides to test content, especially since the publication in 1954 of the American Psychological Association's *Technical Recommendations for Psychological Tests and Diagnostic Techniques*. A good manual describes the test and its development, gives norms for the test, and presents evidence of its validity and reliability. Even test manuals, though, are not objective enough to permit the test user to become careless.

The major reference for critical and objective reviews of most psychological tests is provided by the *Mental Measurements Yearbooks,* edited by Oscar K. Buros. At this writing, there are five bound volumes in the series: the *1938, 1940, Third, Fourth,* and *Fifth;* all are needed, for they are essentially nonduplicative.

Our book is concerned mainly with maximum-performance, objective, supply-response, written, standardized group tests which may be power or speeded and hand- or machine-scored.

Chapter Three # BASIC ATTRIBUTES OF THE TEST

What test should we use? Is Test B better than Test A? Questions like these are really outside the scope of this book. Even so, we should know a little about the characteristics of a good test. We at least should know what to look for when evaluating a test

Three main attributes need to be considered: *validity, reliability,* and *usability*. Validity refers to the ability of the test to do the job we want it to. Reliability means that a test gives dependable or consistent scores. Usability includes all such practical factors as cost, ease of scoring, time required, and the like. These attributes are not absolute, but are relative to specific situations, uses, groups, etc.

Now let us consider each of these attributes in detail.

VALIDITY

Validity is the most important single attribute. Nothing will be gained by testing unless the test has some validity for the use we wish to make of it. A test which has high validity for one purpose may have moderate validity for another, and negligible validity for a third.

> The hypothetical *Mechanical Applications and Practices Test* (MAP) has been found highly valid for predicting grades at the Manual Arts High School and for selection of machinists' apprentices. It has reasonable, but low, validity for predicting performance in a manual training course and for the selection of women for simple industrial assembly jobs. The MAP is of no value, though, in predicting academic grade-point averages, in selecting industrial sales representatives, or in selecting students to enter engineering colleges. The MAP, for some reason that is not immediately apparent, even relates negatively to success in real estate selling; the better salesmen tend to score lower on the test.

There are no fixed rules for deciding what is meant by high validity, moderate validity, etc. Skill in making such decisions comes through training and experience in dealing with tests, and we cannot go into much detail here. We will, however, consider some of the ways of looking at test validity.

Face Validity

One way is through *face validity*. This means simply that the test looks as if it should be valid. Good face validity helps to keep motivation high, for people are likely to try harder when the test seems reasonable. In some situations, too, good face validity is important to public relations.

> According to a recent news item, one state senator has criticized his state's civil service examiners for using this (paraphrased) item in a test for hospital orderlies:
>
> *In what way are a moth and a plant alike?*
>
> The original item comes from an excellent and widely accepted standardized adult intelligence test and is one of a series of items which call for the examinee to detect the essential similarity between two seemingly dissimilar things. Taken by itself, the item has very poor face validity; after all, why should a hospital orderly have to know such a trivial fact as this?

Face validity, though important at times, is not nearly so important as other indications of validity.

Content Validity

Somewhat similar, but at a more sophisticated level, is *content validity* (otherwise known as: logical validity, course validity, curricular validity, or textbook validity). Like face validity, content validity is nonstatistical; here, however, the test content is examined in detail.

> We may check an achievement test to see whether each item covers an important bit of knowledge or involves an important skill related to a particular training program. Or we may start off with a detailed outline of our training program and see how thoroughly the test covers its important points.

Content validity is most obviously important in achievement tests, but it may be important with other types, too.

The term, *factorial validity*, is sometimes used to indicate that a test is a relatively pure measure of some particular characteristic. Factorial indicates that the evidence for its purity comes from factor analysis, a mathematical technique for identifying the basic dimensions causing the interrelationships found among a set of tests.

A test is said to have high factorial validity if it seems to be a good measure of some dimension which has been isolated or identified through a factor analysis. Even if a test does measure a factor well, I do not believe that the evidence should be termed validity because the factor exists only as a statistical artifact. Then, too, factors can be named whatever the factor analyst wishes. If this is validity at all, which I doubt, it is presumably a sort of content validity. Some other writers classify factorial validity by itself or mention it under construct validity (which we shall consider shortly).

Empirical Validity

Empirical validity is implied whenever no adjective is used to modify validity. This is most important in practical situations. How well does the test measure what we want it to in practical situations? Empirical validity gives us the answer by indicating how closely the test relates to some criterion (i.e., to some standard of performance). When empirical validity is high, we can use the test for predicting performance on the criterion variable. Almost anything else can be forgiven if the test has very high empirical validity.

Evidence for this type of validity is gained through a validity coefficient, a coefficient of correlation between the test and a criterion.

A correlation coefficient is a statistic which expresses the tendency for values of two variables to change together systematically. It may take any value between 0.00 (no relationship) and + 1.00 or − 1.00 (each indicating a perfect relationship). Further information on this statistic will be found in Chapter Four.

Factors Influencing Empirical Validity

Skill is required to interpret validity coefficients. In general, the higher the correlation between the test and the criterion, the better; however, many other factors have to be considered:

1. Test Variables Differ

Some tests lend themselves more naturally to validation studies than do others. For example, school grades are a natural criterion to use in validating a scholastic aptitude test. On the other hand, what would we use as a good criterion for an anxiety scale? Where good criteria are hard to find, we usually cannot expect high validity coefficients; sometimes in fact the test may even be a better measure of the characteristic than the criterion is.

2. Criteria Differ

The criterion used in one validation study may be more important or more relevant to our purposes than the criterion used in another validation study.

We want a test to help us in the selection of bookbinders. The *Health Analysis Form* correlates 0.65 with record of attendance; the *Hand Dexterity Test* correlates 0.30 with number of books bound during an observation period. Which test should we use? Should we use both? We would need more information, of course, but we would certainly want to consider which criterion (attendance record or production record) is more pertinent.

3. Groups Differ

For any number of reasons, the test which works well with one group may not do so with another group. The test which discriminates between bright and dull primary school pupils may be worthless when used with high school students because all high school students get near-perfect scores. Consider also:

> The *Aytown Advertiser* finds that the *Typographers Own Performance Scale* (TOPS) is very helpful in selecting good printers and in reducing turnover among printers, but that it is no good in selecting reporters and office workers. *The Beetown Bugle* finds that the TOPS is of little value in selecting its printers. (This is entirely possible, for the two newspapers may have different standards of quality, the labor markets may differ in the two cities, etc.)

4. Variability Differs

Validity coefficients are likely to be higher when the group of examinees shows a wide range of scores. A casual glance may tell us that John (a basketball center) is taller than Bill (who is of average height), but it may take a close look to tell whether Bill is taller than Tom (who is also of average height). In much the same way, a crude test can discriminate well if there are gross differences among those tested, but a much better test may not discriminate adequately if the group is highly homogeneous.

5. Additional Information

A validity coefficient must also be evaluated in terms of how much additional information it will give us. One test may correlate very high with a criterion variable, but still not help us much. This situation is likely to occur whenever the test also correlates very high with information we already have (e.g., scores from another test or previous school grades). In other words, the test will not be helpful unless it contributes something new to our understanding of the examinees. (Note: If this were not so, we could give several different forms of a valid test to each examinee and, eventually, get perfect validity; unfortunately, we would be getting only a very slight increase in validity in this manner by getting successive measures of the same characteristic.)

These five considerations are only illustrative of why we cannot assert flatly, "the higher the validity coefficient, the better." Other things being equal, the statement will be true; however, we must be sure that other things are equal.

Empirical validity may be either concurrent or predictive. Some writers treat these as separate types of validity, but I believe that they are better described as being instances of empirical validity, for they differ only in time sequence. In concurrent validity, both test scores and criterion values are obtained at about the same time. In predictive validity, there is some lapse in time between testing and obtaining the criterion values.

Construct Validity

Construct validity is the fourth and final type that we shall mention here. Like empirical validity, it typically involves a correlation between test scores and values of another variable; however, the outside variable is not really a criterion, even though it is a variable which should relate logically to the test. Construct validity is probably the most important type in psychological theory. In general, construct validity is concerned with the psychological meaningfulness of the test.

> Suppose that we decide to develop a *Social Extraversion Test* (SET) for high school students. We decide that one evidence of extraversion is to be found in participation in school activities. We give the SET to all of the students in our school and check the number of hours per week each student spends on school activities. The correlation coefficient between these two variables will be evidence of construct validity.

With construct validity, we predict the results which logically should be obtained if the test is valid. The prediction is stated concretely enough and precisely enough so that it can be tested statistically. In this way, we actually are checking the validity of both the test and its underlying theory.

Additional sophistication is needed for evaluating construct validities. The concept is mentioned here only for general information. The casual test user will want to study the concept further before attempting to evaluate tests where construct validation is involved.

RELIABILITY

Reliability refers to the consistency of measurement and is important because of its relationship to validity. A test cannot measure anything well unless it measures something consistently; however, a test may measure consistently without measuring well the characteristic in which we are interested.

> I ask my psychology students to run one quarter-mile lap on the university's track. One week later, I have them run another quarter-mile lap. Each student's time is about the same for each of his two runs; therefore, this running test gives reliable results. My students will object, however, if I propose to base their grades on their speed of running because it is not a valid measure of their knowledge of psychology.

Reliability may be assessed in either an absolute or relative sense. Absolute consistency refers to the variability in score that would be expected in any person's performance if he were tested repeatedly with the same test (or parallel forms of the test); this way of viewing reliability in test-score units is expressed through the standard error of measurement which will be considered in Chapter Four. Relative consistency refers to the ability of the test to yield scores which place examinees in the same position relative to each other; this way of viewing reliability is the more common and will be developed in this section. Relative reliability provides us with an index of over-all dependability of scores in the form of a correlation coefficient (a statistic considered in further detail in Chapter Four), known here as a coefficient of reliability.

> If we had a perfectly reliable criterion (possible only in theory, never in practice), the highest validity coefficient we could possibly obtain would be equal to the square root of the test's reliability coefficient.

It is not too important to remember this specific point; however, we do need to remember that reasonably high reliability is necessary for good validity. We need to remember, too, that reliability does not insure validity; reliability is necessary for, but is no guarantee of, validity.

We will consider three dimensions of test reliability: scorer, content, and temporal.

Scorer Reliability

When tests are not scored objectively, *scorer reliability* must be considered. We want evidence that the test will be scored similarly by two (or more) qualified persons and that it will be scored similarly by the same person at different times. With objective tests, there will be perfect scorer reliability if there are no mistakes in the scoring; and we may guard against mistakes by checking our work carefully.

There is much evidence that most supply-response tests (such as the typical essay examinations given in school and college courses) have very low scorer reliability; however, there is also evidence that this reliability can be increased materially by careful preparation of items and by thorough training of graders.

> Twenty teachers were asked to rank a set of ten essays. Six different essays received at least a single vote for rank one. Of these six essays, three were ranked last by at least one other teacher. The grade an essay receives seems to depend more on who grades it than on its inherent quality. Or, as this same thought has been expressed in literature:

> Beauty is in the eye of the beholder!

Content Reliability

The test publisher should offer evidence that his test possesses suitable *content reliability*. This is evidence that the test items are measuring the same thing. Although any two items may be quite independent of each other, all items on the test should be centered on the same general content area, thereby accentuating what they have in common. And if there are several different forms of a test, the publisher should show that these forms yield very similar results. The publisher of one test that is available in several forms states flatly that all forms give the same results. The manual includes only one set of norms; this set is supposed to apply to all forms. In actual fact, there are marked differences among the forms. Some users of the test know that these differences exist and have developed their own norms (a different set for each form); however, others still use the single set supplied by the publisher and must make many unfortunate decisions as they assume that the forms yield interchangeable results.

Provided the test is not highly speeded, evidence of content reliability may be obtained from one administration of a single form of a test. One common way of doing this is through the use of an internal consistency measure such as one of the Kuder-Richardson formulas; these formulas involve detailed assumptions about the test items and total score, but the assumptions are reasonable to make about many tests. The use of an appropriate formula gives a good estimate of the test's content reliability.

Another common way lies through the use of a split-half (sometimes called odd-even) reliability coefficient.

> We score each person's paper twice: once for the odd items only and once for the even items only. We find the correlation between these odd-item and even-item scores; however, this correlation coefficient is an underestimate of the test's reliability, for longer tests tend to be more reliable than shorter ones and we have correlated two half-length tests. Fortunately we can estimate the full-length test's reliability from a formula.

Both the internal-consistency and the split-half approaches make many assumptions that we will not go into here. However, one precaution does seem in order: neither approach may be used when speed is an important factor in determining a person's test score.

> A clerical test consists of pairs of numbers which the examinee must mark as being S (exactly the same) or D (different in some way). The score is the number of items correctly marked in five minutes. The items have almost no difficulty; without a time limit, anyone could obtain a perfect score. Few examinees make any errors. If we split this test into odd and even halves, we will usually have exactly equal scores. Computing a split-half or internal-consistency reliability coefficient for this test would be ridiculous, for the coefficient would be spuriously high. On tests such as this, examinees differ in the speed with which they can do the tasks, not in their ability to do the work that is called for.

Temporal Reliability (Test-Retest)

The third major dimension of reliability is *stability over time*. A test cannot give valid results if it gives different scores at different times. *Temporal reliability* is assessed by giving the same test to the same group at two different times, and by correlating scores made on the first and second testings. A reliability coefficient obtained in this fashion is generally a fair indication of the test's reliability; however, there are some shortcomings, too.

If the second administration is given very shortly after the first, some people may remember specific items—and this will influence the results. With some kinds of tests, the difficulty level of the items is changed considerably once a person has taken the test, as, for example, when much of the difficulty depends on having the examinee figure out how to work some type of problem. If the time interval between testings is very long, real changes may have taken place in the examinees and test scores should be different; in such situations, the ability of the test to reflect these real changes in the people will result in a spuriously low reliability coefficient, because the changes in score are not the fault of the test. For example:

> Fourth-grade pupils are tested at the beginning and retested at the end of the school year; all pupils will have learned something, but some will have learned much more than others. Inexperienced machinists, retested after six months on the job, will show the same sort of pattern—some men having changed appreciably, some having changed little. People undergoing psychotherapy between first and second testing may show markedly different scores.

Factors Affecting Reliability

Thousands of pages have been written on test reliability; however, we will do little more here than suggest a few of the factors which influence reliability.

1. Length Increases Reliability

The longer the test, the more reliable it will be—provided other factors are held constant (for example, that the group tested is the same, that the new items are as good as those on the shorter test, and that the test does not become so long that fatigue is a consideration). I will illustrate this point with an analogy.

Consider a major national golf tournament, one which extends over several days. A relatively unknown golfer often is leading at the end of the first day, but the eventual winner is nearly always a well-known figure. Although any golfer in the tournament may have a single "hot" round, it is the expert who can be depended upon in the long run. In the same way, chance plays a much greater role in influencing test scores on short tests than on longer ones.

2. Heterogeneity Increases Reliability

The variability of the group tested is also important in evaluating any reliability coefficient. If everything else is the same, higher reliability coefficients will be found for groups which vary more in ability. Let us illustrate this point with an absurd example.

We are going to demonstrate the reliability of a *Reading Speed Test* (RST). From our school system, we select at random, one pupil from each grade, one through nine. We test each child in this sample; one week later, we test them again. Inasmuch as speed of reading increases markedly through these grades, we should have a tremendous range in scores—and the differences among pupils should be so great that order of score is not likely to change from one administration of the test to the next. The reliability coefficient, then, would prove to be very high. If, on the other hand, we were to select a small group of average ability second-graders and test them twice (as above) on the RST, we should find a very low reliability coefficient; these pupils probably would not differ much in their initial scores—and order of score might very well change on the second testing, thereby reducing the reliability coefficient.

We need to study carefully the publisher's description of the group used and the conditions of testing in any reliability report.

3. Shorter Time, Higher Reliability

The length of time between the two testings in a test-retest reliability coefficient is of obvious importance. As we would expect, reliability is higher when the time between the two testings is short. This is the reason that IQ's change most when there is a long period of time between testings.

4. Irregularities Reduce Reliability

Irregular testing conditions tend to lower reliability coefficients. Failure to follow directions for giving the test (e.g., allowing too much time) may make a considerable difference on some tests. Unfavorable physical conditions (e.g., a hot, poorly ventilated, ill-lighted room) will reduce reliability, for some people may be affected more than others. Personal illness, uneven motivation, and cheating are among other common irregularities, for they are all conditions which will influence some scores more than others.

Comparing Validity and Reliability

Validity is established through a statistical comparison of scores with values on some outside variable. Any constant error in the test will have a direct adverse effect on the test's validity.

> We want to select power sewing machine operators. We use a test which contains many difficult words that are not related to sewing machine operation. Since this extraneous factor will influence each individual's score in a consistent fashion, the hard words will reduce the test's validity for our purpose. (Note that the reliability is not necessarily reduced.)

No outside variable is involved in reliability, for reliability is not concerned with what a test measures—only with the consistency with which it measures. As noted above, irregularities in testing procedures have a direct and adverse effect on reliability; indirectly, they may reduce validity as well. (Note: These irregularities are known as variable errors. Variable here simply means nonconstant. In most other places throughout this book, variable is a general term referring to any characteristic, test, or the like, which may assume different values.)

USABILITY

The third basic attribute of a test is *usability*. We include here all the many practical factors that go into our decision to use a particular test. Let me give one more imaginary example.

> We are wondering whether to use the *Lyman Latin Verb Test* (LLVT) or the *Latin Original Verb Examination* (LOVE) in our

high school Latin course. Since both tests are hypothetical, we may give them any characteristics we desire. My LLVT, therefore, has perfect reliability and validity. The LOVE, while not perfect, does have respectable validity and reliability for our purposes. We'll probably decide to use the LOVE in spite of the LLVT's perfection, for the LLVT takes two weeks to administer and an additional week to score, can be given to only one examinee at a time, costs $1000 per examinee, and can be administered and scored by only one person. The LOVE, on the other hand, can be given to a group of students simultaneously, has reusable test booklets which cost only ten cents per copy (answer sheets cost three cents apiece), and can be scored by a clerical worker in two or three minutes.

Under usability, we deal with all sorts of practical considerations. A longer test may be more reliable, even more valid; however, if we have only a limited time for testing, we may have to compromise with the ideal. If the preferred test is too expensive, we may have to buy another one instead (or buy fewer copies of the first test), and so on.

I am not suggesting that validity and reliability are important only in theory. They are vitally important. After all, there is no point in testing unless we can have some confidence in the results. Practical factors must be considered, but only if the test has satisfactory reliability and validity.

Chapter Four A FEW

STATISTICS

It is too bad that so many people are afraid of or bored by statistics. Statistics is a fascinating subject with a lurid history. Professional gamblers are among many who have found the study very
profitable. More important right here, I suppose, is the fact that
elementary statistics is easy to understand. If you have completed
ninth-grade mathematics, you should have little trouble in grasp-
ing the basic fundamentals.

INTRODUCTION

Some of the points in this chapter will be a little clearer if we
start off with a concrete example.

Fifty men who applied for jobs at the Knifty Knife Korporation
took the *Speedy Signal Test*. They obtained the following scores
(where one point was given for each correct answer):

AA	38	AK	35	AU	34	BE	32	BO	30
AB	43	AL	36	AV	36	BF	37	BP	30
AC	36	AM	37	AW	33	BG	29	BQ	36
AD	31	AN	35	AX	35	BH	33	BR	25
AE	25	AO	37	AY	37	BI	35	BS	42
AF	28	AP	31	AZ	33	BJ	34	BT	38
AG	38	AQ	34	BA	35	BK	31	BU	41
AH	35	AR	34	BB	35	BL	32	BV	27
AI	31	AS	26	BC	41	BM	34	BW	37
AJ	35	AT	28	BD	33	BN	30	BX	32

Continuous and Discrete Variables

We treat test scores as if they were *continuous*. Continuous values are the results of measuring, rather than counting. We cannot have absolute accuracy, for we might always use still finer instruments to obtain greater precision. We can measure relatively tangible variables such as length and weight with considerable accuracy, but we find it harder to measure accurately such intangibles as intelligence, aptitude, and neuroticism. The principle is the same, though: absolute precision of measurement is not possible with any variable. The degree of accuracy depends on the nature of the variable itself, the precision of the instrument, and the nature of the situation.

> See how this works with *length*. In discussing the size of my office, I may use dimensions accurate to the nearest foot. I may note my desk size to the nearest inch. I measure the height of my children to the nearest quarter-inch. My model builder friends do work that is accurate to the nearest one sixty-fourth inch, and scientists working on our rockets and satellites need even greater precision.

Some variables take only discrete values. Here we count, and complete accuracy is possible: number of volumes in the public libraries of Ohio, number of students in each classroom at Walnut Grove High School, number of cabbages in San Francisco supermarkets, etc. The tipoff, usually, is in the phrase "number of." When the variable can be expressed in that way, we usually have a discrete variable.

If we think of a test as only a collection of questions and of test scores as only the number of items correct, we will have to consider test scores as discrete values. We do often obtain our scores by counting the number of correct answers; however, we usually want to consider the test scores as measures of some characteristic beyond the test itself.

> We are not satisfied with thinking of AA merely as having answered correctly thirty-eight items on his *Speedy Signal Test*. Rather, we want to consider this 38 as an indication of some amount of the ability which underlies the test.

Any test is only a sample of the items that might have been included. We hope that the test is a representative sample of this universe (or population) of all possible items. The universe of possible items for most tests is almost infinite, for we could not possibly write all of the items which would be relevant. We find it helpful to think of any psychological or educational test as being a rather crude instrument for measuring whatever characteristic (ability, knowledge, aptitude, interest, etc.) is presumed to underlie the test. Although not everyone agrees, most test authorities treat test scores as continuous. And we shall do so in this book, for continuous scores can be handled mathematically in ways that discrete values cannot.

The Histogram

Let us return to our example of the fifty applicants for employment at the Knifty Knife Korporation. We may show the results graphically by marking off all possible score values (within the range actually made) along a horizontal line. This horizontal line, called the *abscissa*, will serve as the baseline of our graph. If we use a tiny square to represent each applicant, we will have a graph like that shown in Figure 1. Since these scores are continuous, we let each of those little squares occupy the space of one full unit; that is,

Figure 1.

each square occupies a space from 0.5 below the stated score value to 0.5 above the stated score value. AA's score was 38; his square is placed so that it extends from 37.5 to 38.5 (the real limits of the score), thereby having half of its area above and half below 38.0 (the midpoint of the score). We can tell the number of cases (the frequency) falling at any specified score by counting the number of squares above it or, even more simply, by reading the number on the ordinate (the vertical axis) of the graph at a height level with the top of the column. This is called a *histogram*.

When we draw a graph to show a set of scores, we ordinarily make no effort to retain the identity of the individuals. We are less interested in knowing AA's score or AB's score than we are in portraying the general nature of the scores made by the group. We are likely to be interested in general characteristics such as the shape of the distribution, the scores obtained most frequently, the range in scores, etc. Ordinarily, therefore, we would be more likely to draw the histogram in one of the ways shown in Figure 2. Here

Figure 2.

we have no need for individual squares; instead, we draw columns (each one unit wide) to the height required to show appropriate frequency.

Frequency Distribution and Class Intervals

We sometimes find it convenient to group adjacent scores together. For example, we might measure the length of each of one hundred objects to the nearest inch, but prefer to group the measurements into intervals of six inches or one foot when showing them graphically.

We often do this same thing when graphing test results. For the sake of illustration, we will take the same fifty test scores reported on page 39 and arrange them into a frequency distribution as in Table 1. At the left, we have retained the original score values— each unit, therefore, is equal to one score value. At the right, however, we have arranged the scores into class intervals which are two

TABLE 1

SPEEDY SIGNAL TEST SCORES OF THE FIFTY KNIFTY KNIFE KORPORATION'S APPLICANTS

(1) Score Expressed as:	(2) Real Limits of Score	(3) Midpoint of Score	(4) Frequency (f)	(5) Class Intervals of 2	(6) Real Limits of Interval	(7) Midpoint of Interval	(8) Frequency (f)
43	42.5-43.5	43.0	1	43-44	42.5-44.5	43.5	1
42	41.5-42.5	42.0	1				
41	40.5-41.5	41.0	2	41-42	40.5-42.5	41.5	3
40	39.5-40.5	40.0	0				
39	38.5-39.5	39.0	0	39-40	38.5-40.5	39.5	0
38	37.5-38.5	38.0	3				
37	36.5-37.5	37.0	5	37-38	36.5-38.5	37.5	8
36	35.5-36.5	36.0	4				
35	34.5-35.5	35.0	8	35-36	34.5-36.5	35.5	12
34	33.5-34.5	34.0	5				
33	32.5-33.5	33.0	4	33-34	32.5-34.5	33.5	9
32	31.5-32.5	32.0	3				
31	30.5-31.5	31.0	4	31-32	30.5-32.5	31.5	7
30	29.5-30.5	30.0	3				
29	28.5-29.5	29.0	1	29-30	28.5-30.5	29.5	4
28	27.5-28.5	28.0	2				
27	26.5-27.5	27.0	1	27-28	26.5-28.5	27.5	3
26	25.5-26.5	26.0	1				
25	24.5-25.5	25.0	2	25-26	24.5-26.5	25.5	3

score values wide. Ordinarily we would use either individual score values or class intervals, not both. The essential information is contained in columns 1 and 4 or columns 5 and 8. The remaining columns are included only for the guidance of the reader.

In the last paragraph, we encountered two new terms: *frequency distribution* and *class interval.* A frequency distribution is any orderly arrangement of scores, usually from high to low, showing the frequency with which each score value (or class interval of scores) occurs when some specified group is tested. A class interval is the unit used within a frequency distribution (although we rarely call it a class interval if the unit is only a single score value). The use of class intervals provides a means of grouping together several adjacent score values so that they may be treated as alike for computational or graphing purposes. We assume that all of the cases in a particular class interval fall at the midpoint of that interval except when we're computing the median or other percentiles (where we assume that the cases are spread evenly across the interval). The midpoint seems self-descriptive: it is that value which lies halfway between the real limits of the interval.

When used with test scores, class intervals must be of the same width (size) throughout any given distribution. We cannot use class intervals two score values wide at one place and five score values wide at another place in the same distribution.

Usually, when selecting a class interval width we select an odd number, so that the midpoints of our class intervals will be integers (whole numbers). Note that when we used 2 as our class interval width in Table 1, our midpoints were not whole numbers (e.g., the midpoint of the class interval 43-44, is 43.5). This always happens when a class interval is not an odd number of score values in width. As a general rule, we try to make our intervals of such a width that we will have a total of about fifteen intervals—somewhat more, perhaps, when we have a great many scores, and somewhat fewer when we have very few scores.

We must now differentiate score limits and real limits. Score limits are simply the extreme integral score values which are included in a given class interval. Real limits are the upper and lower extremities. See Table 1, and check the following illustration:

> A class interval of 21–25 means that 21 and 25 are the score limits; scores of 21, 22, 23, 24, and 25 are included in this interval.

The real limits extend from the real lower limit of the lowest score (20.5) to the real upper limit of the highest score (25.5). As a check to see that the interval is five units wide: $25.5 - 20.5 = 5.0$; as a double check, note that five different integral score values (21, 22, 23, 24, and 25) fall within the interval.

In drawing a histogram, we make the sides of the upright columns extend to the real limits of each score (or class interval). The height of each column depends on the frequency (the number of people making each score); thus we can tell the number of people who made any specified score by reading the number on the ordinate opposite the top of the column.

Frequency Polygon

Another type of graph which may be used for the same purpose is the frequency polygon. A dot is placed above the midpoint of each score value (or each class interval) at a height which corresponds to the number of people making that score. Each of these dots is connected with the two adjacent dots by straight lines. In addition, the distribution is extended one unit (i.e., either one score value or one class interval) beyond the highest and lowest scores obtained. This means that there will be lines to the baseline at each extreme, thereby completing the figure and making our graph a polygon (a many-sided figure).

Figure 3 is a frequency polygon showing the test scores of the fifty Knifty Knife Korporation applicants; we have used class intervals which are two score values wide and show the information in columns 5 and 8 of Table 1.

It can be shown mathematically, although we will not do so here, that a histogram and a frequency polygon showing the same data and drawn to the same scale, are identical in area. This is important—for it is customary when drawing graphs to make area proportional to frequency of cases. (The fact that height is also proportional to frequency results from our having score-units equally spaced along the abscissa.)

We may use the histogram and the frequency polygon interchangeably except when we need to compare the distributions of two or more groups. In such instances, we nearly always use the frequency polygon since it will be easier to read.

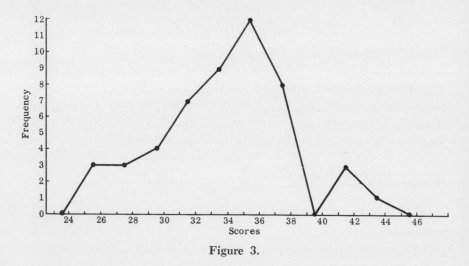

Figure 3.

Figure 4 shows the distribution of the fifty Knifty Knife applicants compared with the distribution of fifty-two present employees of the Knifty Knife Korporation.

Figure 4. SST Scores of 52 Knifty Knife Employees and of 50 Applicants for Employment.

[Please note: If the number of cases were not very nearly the same in each of the groups, we would have to use percentages (rather than frequencies) on the ordinate so that the areas under each polygon would be the same and a direct visual comparison could be made.]

DESCRIPTIVE STATISTICS

Graphs are very helpful in giving us a general impression of a distribution. After a little practice, we can learn a great deal from a graph. Descriptive statistics, however, provide a more precise means for summarizing or describing a set of scores. Descriptive statistics include measures of position (including central tendency), measures of variability, and measures of covariability.

Measures of Position (Other Than Central Tendency)

Measures of position are numbers which tell us where a specified person or a particular score value stands within a set of scores. In a graph, any measure of position is located as a point on the baseline.

Rank

Rank is the simplest description of position—first for the best or highest; second for the next best; third, etc. on to last. Its assets are its familiarity and its simplicity; however, its interpretation is so dependent on the size of the group that it is less useful than one might think at first. We use it only informally in describing test results.

Percentile Rank

Percentile rank is a better position indicator because it makes allowance for difference in size of group. Percentile rank is a statement of a person's relative position within a defined group—thus a percentile rank of 38 indicates a score that is as high as or higher than those made by 38 per cent of the people in that particular group. Percentile ranks are widely used as a type of test score. They will be considered in detail in Chapter Six.

Measures of Central Tendency

A measure of central tendency is designed to give us a single value which is most characteristic or typical of a set of scores. Three such measures are fairly common in testing: the mean, median, and mode. Each of these may be located as a point along the baseline of a graph.

Mean

The most common measure of position and of central tendency is the *arithmetic mean* (usually called simply the mean). This is nothing more than the average we learned in elementary school. But average is a generic term and may refer to any measure of central tendency. The mean is the preferred measure for general use with test scores. Besides certain mathematical advantages, the mean is widely understood and easy to compute. We use the mean unless there is good reason to prefer the median.

In grade school we learned to find the mean by adding up all the scores and dividing by the number of scores. Stated as a formula, this becomes:

$\overline{X} = \Sigma X/N$, where
$\overline{X}$ = the mean of Test X
Σ = "to add"
X = raw score on Test X
N = number of cases (number of persons for whom we have scores).

Median

Do you make $100,000 a year? Let us assume that you do. The four other men who live on your street earn $10,000 each. What is the average annual income of the male residents on your street?

$$1 \times \$100,000 = \$100,000$$
$$4 \times \quad 10,000 = \underline{\quad 40,000}$$
$$\$140,000$$

$$\overline{X} = \frac{\Sigma X}{N}$$

$$= \frac{\$140,000}{5}$$

$$= \$28,000$$

But $28,000 is not a very good indication of *central* tendency, is it? With income data, we are likely to have one very high salary (or, at best, a very few high salaries) and many more lower salaries. The result is that the mean tends to exaggerate the salaries (that is, it pulls toward the extreme values) and the median becomes the preferred measure. The *median* is that value above which fall 50 per cent of the cases and below which fall 50 per cent of the cases; thus it is less likely to be drawn in the direction of the extreme cases.

Income data is usually positively skewed—having many low values and a few very high values. This same sort of distribution, shown in Figure 5(a), is frequently found when a test is too difficult or when the examinees are not well prepared. Figure 5(b) is nega-

Figure 5. Three Nonsymmetrical Distributions.

tively skewed, the sort of distribution we are likely to get when a test is too easy for the group tested. The mean gives us an erroneous impression of central tendency whenever a distribution is badly skewed, and the median becomes the preferred measure.

The median is also preferred whenever a distribution is truncated (cut off in some way so that there are no cases beyond a certain point). In Figure 5(c), the distribution is truncated, perhaps because of a very difficult test on which zero was the lowest score given; the dotted line suggests the distribution we might have obtained if the scoring had allowed negative scores.

Since the median is the fiftieth percentile (also the second quartile and the fifth decile), it is the logical measure of central tendency to use when percentile ranks are being used.

Mode

The third type of average used with test scores is the *mode*. The

mode is the most commonly obtained score or the midpoint of the
score interval which has the highest frequency.

The mode is less often usable in connection with further com-
putations than either the mean or the median. It is very easily found,
however, and we can use it as a quick indication of central tendency.
If the scores are arranged in a frequency distribution, the mode is
equal to the midpoint of the score (or class interval) which has the
highest frequency. If a distribution of scores is graphed, the mode
is even more quickly found—for it will be the highest point of the
curve, as shown in Figure 6. Sometimes there are two modes (bi-

Figure 6.   The Mode.

modal) or even more (multimodal) to a distribution. Graphs (c)
and (d) in Figure 6 are both bimodal, even though the peaks in
Graph (d) are not quite of equal height.

Comparison of the Central Tendency Measures

Let us recapitulate quickly.

The mean is the best measure of central tendency to use in most
testing situations. We use it unless there is some good reason not to.
It is widely understood and fairly easily computed. It fits logically
and mathematically into the computation of other statistics. On
the other hand, the mean should not be used when the distribution of scores is badly skewed or truncated, because it is not a good
indicator of central tendency in such situations.

The median fits logically into the percentile scale. Its use is
preferred whenever distributions are badly skewed or truncated.
It involves fewer mathematical assumptions than the mean. Although less widely used than the mean, it is easily understood.

The mode is less widely used than either the mean or the median.
It provides a quick and easy estimate of central tendency, but it is
not especially useful in connection with test scores.

There are still other measures of central tendency, but none is commonly used in testing.

Any measure of central tendency can be located as a point along the abscissa of a graph.

Measures of Variability

It is possible for two distributions of scores to have similar (even identical) central tendency values and yet be very different. The scores in one distribution, for example, may be spread out over a far greater range of values than those in the other distribution. These next statistics tell us how much *variability* (or dispersion) there is in a distribution; that is, they tell us how scattered or spread out the scores are. In graphic work, each of these measures is represented by a distance along the baseline.

Range

The *range* is familiar to all of us, representing the difference between highest and lowest scores. The range is easily found and easily understood, but is valuable only as a rough indication of variability.

It is the least stable measure of variability, depending entirely on the two most extreme (and, therefore, least typical) scores. It is less useful in connection with other statistics than other measures of variability.

Semi-Interquartile Range

This statistic defines itself: *Semi* (half) *inter* (between) *quartile* (one of three points dividing the distribution into four groups of equal size) *range* (difference or distance); in other words, the statistic equals one-half the distance between the extreme quartiles, Q_3 (seventy-fifth percentile) and Q_1 (twenty-fifth percentile).

We use the semi-interquartile range as a measure of dispersion whenever we use the median as the measure of central tendency. It is preferred to other measures when a distribution of scores is truncated or badly skewed. It is sometimes useful when describing the variability of a set of scores to nonprofessionals. The formula for the semi-interquartile range is:

$$Q = \frac{Q_3 - Q_1}{2} \text{, where}$$

Q = semi-interquartile range
Q_3 = third quartile, the seventy-fifth percentile (P_{75})
Q_1 = first quartile, the twenty-fifth percentile (P_{25}).

Average Deviation (Mean Deviation)

Another statistic which has been used to express variability is the *average deviation* or *mean deviation*. Its chief advantage is the simplicity of its rationale, for it is simply the mean absolute amount by which scores differ from the mean score; however, it is more difficult to compute than some better measures of variability and is seldom used today. It is mentioned only because there are occasional references to it in testing literature.

The Standard Deviation

Although it lacks the obvious rationale of the preceding measures of variability, the *standard deviation* is the best such measure. It is the most dependable measure of variability, for it varies less than other measures from one sample to the next. It fits mathematically with other statistics. It is widely accepted as the best measure of variability, and is of special value to test users because it is the basis for: (1) standard scores; (2) a way of expressing the reliability of a test score; (3) a way of indicating the accuracy of values predicted from a correlation coefficient; and (4) a common statistical test of significance. This statistic, in short, is one which every test user should know thoroughly.

The standard deviation is equal to the square root of the mean of the squared deviations from the distribution's mean. (Read that last sentence again—it is not really that hard!) Although more efficient formulas exist, the standard deviation may be found from the following formula:

$$s_x = \sqrt{\frac{\Sigma(X - \overline{X})^2}{N}} \text{ , where}$$

$s_x =$ standard deviation of Test X
$\sqrt{} =$ "take the square root of"
$\Sigma =$ "to add"
$X =$ raw score on Test X
$\overline{X} =$ mean of Test X
$N =$ number of persons whose scores are involved.

What does the standard deviation mean? After we have found it, what is it all about? As a measure of variability it can be expressed as a distance along the baseline of a graph. The standard deviation is often used as a unit in expressing the difference between two specified score values; differences expressed in this fashion are more comparable from one distribution to another than they would be if expressed as raw scores.

The standard deviation is also frequently used in making interpretations from the normal curve. In a normal distribution, 34.13 per cent of the area under the curve lies between the mean and a point that is one standard deviation away from it; 68.26 per cent of the area lies between a point that is one standard deviation below the mean and a point one standard deviation above the mean. In nonnormal distributions (and perfect normality is never achieved), the figure will not be exactly 68.26 per cent, but it will be approximately two-thirds for most distributions of test scores. In other words, approximately two-thirds of the area (and two-thirds of the cases, for area represents number of persons) will fall within one standard deviation of the mean in most distributions; approximately one-third of the cases will be more than one standard deviation away from the mean.

Measures of Covariability

Measures of *covariability* tell us the extent of the relationship between two tests (or other variables). There is a wide variety of correlation methods, but we shall consider only two of them here: the Pearson product-moment correlation coefficient and the Spearman rank-difference correlation coefficient.

Correlation is the degree of relationship between two (or, in specialized techniques, even more) variables. A correlation coefficient is an index number which expresses the degree of relationship; it may take any value from 0.00 (no relationship) to + 1.00 (perfect positive correlation) or − 1.00 (perfect negative correlation). Let us take three extreme (and impractical) examples to illustrate correlation.

In (a) of Figure 7, we see a perfect positive correlation. Ten students have taken a math test. Their scores are shown as Number Right across the abscissa and as Per Cent Right along the ordinate. Each dot in this scatter diagram represents one student's score according to both number right and per cent right. Since there is a perfect correlation, the dots fall along a straight line. Since the correlation is positive, the dots proceed from lower left to upper right.

In (b) of Figure 7, we see a perfect negative correlation. Here we

Figure 7. **Scatter Diagrams Showing Different Relationships Between Two Variables.**

have the same ten students with their test scores as Number Right (across the abscissa) and Number Wrong (along the ordinate). The dots fall along a straight line, but proceed from upper left to lower right as is characteristic of negative correlations.

There is no regular order to the dots in (c) of Figure 7, for this is a correlation coefficient of 0.00—no correlation at all, either positive or negative. Once again, the Number Right is shown along the abscissa, but this time we have shown Height of Student along the ordinate. Apparently, there is no tendency for math scores and heights to be related.

We will never encounter a perfect correlation in actual practice.

Only rarely are we likely to encounter any correlation coefficients above 0.90 except as reliability coefficients (*see* Reliability in Chapter Three). Validity coefficients (*see* Validity in Chapter Three) are much more likely to run between about 0.20 and 0.60 depending upon the test, the criterion, and the variability in scores within the group tested.

Figure 8 shows a correlation coefficient of approximately 0.50. This is the sort of scatter diagram we might reasonably expect to find for the correlation between a test and its criterion; in fact, such

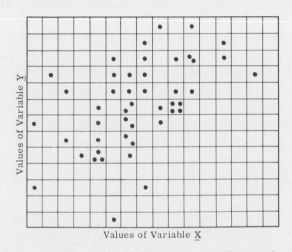

Values of Variable X

Figure 8. Scatter Diagram Showing Correlation Coefficient of Approximately 0.50 Between Variable X and Variable Y.

a correlation may be a reasonably good validity coefficient. Note, however, that we would not be able to predict specific criterion values very efficiently from the test scores. If we could, there would be very little variation in scores within any one of the columns; or, stated differently, all scores in any column would tend to be located very close together.

Although the correlation coefficient states the extent to which values of one variable tend to change systematically with changes in value of a second variable, correlation is not evidence of causation. Two variables may be related without either one causing change in the other.

Here is a simple illustration of the principle that correlation is not proof of causation—an example that is not original with me, although I do not recall the source:

> Among elementary school pupils, there is a positive correlation between length of index finger and mental age. In other words, the longer the index finger, the higher the mental age. Before you start using length of index finger as a test of intelligence (or begin to stretch your child's finger), wait a minute! Do you suppose that higher intelligence causes the longer finger, or vice versa? Neither, of course. Among elementary school children, higher chronological ages result both in higher mental ages and in longer fingers.

As mentioned earlier, we shall consider here only the Pearson product-moment correlation coefficient (r) and the Spearman rank-difference correlation coefficient (rho). The product-moment correlation is computed when both variables are measured continuously and certain specified assumptions can be made. The rank-difference correlation may be employed when the data are expressed as ranks, rather than scores; rank coefficients (there are others besides Spearman's) are somewhat less efficient, but often are reasonably good estimates of r. The formulas for these two types of correlation are given here only for the sake of illustration.

$$r_{xy} = \frac{\Sigma(X - \overline{X})(Y - \overline{Y})}{Ns_x s_y} \text{ , where}$$

r_{xy} = product-moment correlation coefficient
Σ = "to add"
X = raw score on Variable X
$\overline{X}$ = mean of Variable X
Y = raw score on Variable Y
$\overline{Y}$ = mean of Variable Y
N = number of pairs of scores
s_x = standard deviation of Variable X
s_y = standard deviation of Variable Y.

and:

$$rho = 1 - \frac{6\Sigma D^2}{N(N^2 - 1)} \text{ , where}$$

rho = rank-difference correlation coefficient
Σ = "to add"
D = difference between a person's rank on
     Variable X and Variable Y
N = number of cases.

Although there are special correlation techniques where this is not true, most correlation methods demand that we have pairs of score.

> We want to find a validity coefficient of the hypothetical *Industrial Index* by correlating its scores with criterion values (number of units produced during a four-hour period of work). We have test scores for seventy-nine men and criterion information on seventy-four men. The greatest number on whom we could possibly compute our correlation coefficient would be seventy-four; however, if some of the seventy-four men did not take the test we will have an even smaller number with which to work.

As noted in Chapter Three, correlation coefficients are widely used in testing to express validity (where test scores are correlated with criterion values) and reliability (where two scores for the same test are correlated).

THE NORMAL PROBABILITY CURVE

So far we have been discussing obtained distributions. Now it is time to consider a theoretical distribution: the normal probability distribution, the graphical representation of which is known to us as the *normal curve* (*see* Figure 9). We will never obtain a distribution exactly like it, for it is based on an infinite number of observations which vary by pure chance. Nevertheless many human characteristics do seem to be distributed in much this way, and most tests yield distributions which approximate this model when given to large numbers of people.

We find it convenient to treat variables as if they were normally distributed when our results are not grossly asymmetrical, because all the properties of this mathematical model are known. If different obtained distributions approach this same model, we have a better basis for comparisons than we would have otherwise.

The normal curve is important, then, because: (1) it is a mathematical model whose properties are known completely; (2) it is a model which is approached by the distributions of many human characteristics and most test scores; (3) it is relevant to an understanding of certain inferential statistics; and, (4) it gives a basis for understanding the relationship between different types of test score.

CHART 1

In the normal probability curve:

1. The curve is bilaterally symmetrical; i.e., the left and right halves are mirror images of each other. (Therefore, the mean and median have the same value.)
2. The curve is highest in the middle of the distribution. (Therefore, the mode is equal to the mean and the median.)
3. The limits of the curve are plus and minus infinity. (Therefore, the tails of the curve will never quite touch the baseline.)
4. The shape of the curve changes from convex to concave at points one standard deviation above and one below the mean.
5. About 34% (34.13%) of the total area under the curve lies between the mean and a point one standard deviation away. (Since area represents number of cases, about 34% of the examinees have scores which fall between the mean and a point one standard deviation away.)
6. Nearly 48% (47.72%) of the area (nearly 48% of the cases) lies between the mean and a point two standard deviations away.
7. Nearly 49.9% (49.87%) of the area (and the cases) lies between the mean and a point three standard deviations away.
8. About 68% (68.26%) of the area (and the cases) lies within one standard deviation (plus and minus) of the mean. (This was found by doubling the 34% in Number 5, above. In the same way, the percentages in Numbers 7 and 8 may be doubled to find the percentage of area or cases lying within two and three standard deviations of the mean, respectively.)
9. A known mathematical formula describes the curve exactly.
10. Tables exist giving all sorts of information: height of the ordinate at any distance (in standard-deviation units) from the mean, percentage of total area between any two points, etc.

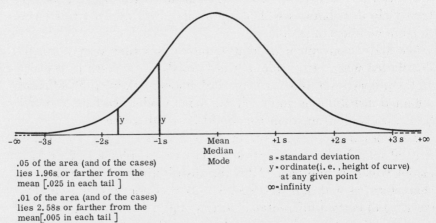

.05 of the area (and of the cases) lies 1.96s or farther from the mean [.025 in each tail]

.01 of the area (and of the cases) lies 2.58s or farther from the mean[.005 in each tail]

s = standard deviation
y = ordinate(i. e. , height of curve) at any given point
∞ = infinity

Figure 9. The Normal Probability Curve.

Points to Know

Chart I and Figure 9 constitute a summary of information about the normal probability curve that every test user should know. These points are worth remembering—even if we have to memorize them!

INFERENTIAL STATISTICS

Inferential statistics (sometimes called sampling or probability statistics) tell us how much confidence may be placed in our descriptive statistics. Whereas descriptive statistics are values used to summarize a set of values, inferential statistics are used to answer the question "so what?" about descriptive statistics. They can be used to tell whether a statistic based on only a sample of cases is probably a close estimate of the value we would find for the entire population, whether the observed difference between means for two groups is probably due to chance alone, etc.

Standard Errors

Space will not permit us to go into much detail on inferential statistics; however, we must develop one concept thoroughly: the *standard error* (especially, the standard error of measurement and the standard error of estimate).

Every descriptive statistic has its standard error although some are rarely used and a few have not yet been worked out by statisticians. A standard error may be thought of as an estimate of the standard deviation of a set of like statistics; it expresses how much variation we might expect if we were to compute the same statistic on many more sample groups just like the one we are working with.

Although the formulas for the different standard errors vary somewhat according to the statistic, most standard errors become smaller (which is what we want) when the number of cases is large and when there is little variability in a set of scores (or a high correlation between sets of scores).

We will illustrate the standard error concept with the *standard error of the mean,* which is found through the formula:

$$SE_{\bar{x}} = \sqrt{\frac{s}{N-1}} \text{ , where}$$

$SE_{\bar{x}}$ = standard error of the mean of Test X
s = standard deviation of Test X
$\sqrt{\ }$ = "take the square root of"
N = number of cases.

Let us say that we give the *Task Test* to each man in one hundred different samples of fifty employees each; for each sample, men are selected randomly from among the 8,000 working at the same job at Giant Enterprises. We compute the mean for each of these one hundred samples. We compute a standard deviation for this distribution of one hundred means by using each mean exactly as if it were a raw score. The standard error of the mean ($SE_{\bar{x}}$), based on only one sample, gives us an estimate of this standard deviation of a set of means. This $SE_{\bar{x}}$ tells how much the mean is likely to vary from one sample to the next.

Suppose now that we have only one random sample of fifty men. The mean is 85.0; the standard deviation is 28.0; the standard error of the mean is 4.0. We want to estimate the mean of the 8,000 Giant Enterprises workers. Our sample mean is an unbiased, honest estimate of the mean of the population (here, our 8,000 men); but we do not know whether our sample mean is higher or lower than the population mean. At least theoretically the value of the population mean is fixed and invariable at any given point in time, even though we don't know what its value is.

It can be shown that when a large number of random samples of the same size are selected from a population, the means of the samples tend to be distributed normally with a grand mean which is equal to the population's mean; the $SE_{\bar{x}}$ is an estimate of what the standard deviation of that distribution would be.

Go back to page 58 and look at the normal curve.

The situation at this point is this: we may consider our sample mean as one observation in a normal distribution which has a standard deviation of 4.0. How close is our sample mean of 85.0 to the population mean?

Since 68 per cent of the area of a normal curve is within one standard deviation of the mean, there are about sixty-eight chances in one hundred that our mean is no more than one standard deviation away from the population mean. It follows that we may be about 68 per cent confident that the population mean is not more than one $SE_{\bar{x}}$ from the sample mean—85.0 ± 4.0, or between 81.0 and 89.0.

Through similar reasoning, we might have about 95 per cent confidence that the population mean has a value not more than ± 1.96 $SE_{\bar{x}}$ away from the sample mean; or 99 per cent confidence that the population mean is not more than ± 2.58 $SE_{\bar{x}}$ away from the sample mean.

Standard Error of Measurement

We use a similar line of reasoning when we use the *standard error of measurement* (SE_{meas}). This statistic indicates how much we would expect a person's score to vary if he were examined repeatedly with the same test (assuming that no learning occurs).

The standard error of measurement is a way of expressing a test's reliability in an absolute sense; that is, not in general or relative terms as with a reliability coefficient (*see* Chapter Three), but in terms of score units. As test users, we should not have to compute this statistic ourselves—unless, of course, we want to verify that the SE_{meas} for our group is comparable to that reported by the test publisher. The formula is:

$$SE_{meas} = s_x \sqrt{1 - r_{xx}}, \text{ where}$$
$$SE_{meas} = \text{standard error of measurement}$$
$$s_x = \text{standard deviation of Test X}$$
$$\sqrt{} = \text{"take the square root of"}$$
$$r_{xx} = \text{a reliability coefficient for Test X.}$$

Let us take an example:

Yung Youngdahl gets a score of 73 on an aptitude test. How close is this obtained score to Yung's true score? We use the SE_{meas} in much the same way we did the $SE_{\bar{x}}$ to set up confidence limits for his true score. Thus, we may have about 99 per cent confidence that his true score lies between $73 \pm 2.58 \, SE_{meas}$.

Actually, measurement theory describes the distribution of obtained scores about the theoretical true score, rather than about the obtained score; however, we are not very wrong if we interpret the SE_{meas} as suggested in the preceding paragraph.

The standard error of measurement is extremely important for test users to grasp. It is something we need to keep in mind at all times. If we assume that a person's obtained score is necessarily his true score, we will make all kinds of misinterpretations.

Jim and Jack Johnson are brothers. Jim's IQ, found on a group test taken in the second grade, was 108. Jack's IQ, found on the same test when he was in the second grade, was 111. Jim's score was interpreted as average, but Jack's score was described as above average. According to many IQ classifications, we might very well describe these two IQ's in this fashion. We should note, however, that no test scores are infallible, and that it is entirely possible that the theoretical true scores of Jim and Jack on this test would place them in the reverse order.

Those of us who teach know the difficulty we often have in deciding exactly where to draw the line between *A* and *B* grades, *B* and *C* grades, etc. It is probable that true appraisals (if they were available) of our students would reverse the grades of many borderline students. This is the case with *every* type of score.

Errors, Not Mistakes

It is important to realize that when we speak of *error* here, we are speaking of the error that is inherent in any measurement. It is something with which we must cope whenever we have a continuous variable (described on pages 40-41). Since the term error is a common one in testing, we should know that the following are not errors in a statistical sense:

1. Mistakes in giving test directions
2. Mistakes in timing the test
3. Mistakes in preparing the scoring key
4. Mistakes in scoring
5. Mistakes in recording scores
6. Mistakes in the use of norms tables.

Mistakes must be guarded against. But the error of measurement we are considering here is always with us in testing. We cannot eliminate measurement error, but we can estimate how much error is present. We can eliminate mistakes, but we cannot estimate their extent when they are present.

Because of certain similarities, the standard error of measurement is often confused with the standard error of estimate, the last standard error that we shall consider.

Standard Error of Estimate (SE_{yx})

The purpose of the *standard error of estimate* is to indicate how well test scores predict criterion values. Correlation coefficients give us the basis for predicting values of a criterion from our knowledge of obtained test scores. The SE_{yx} shows how much predicted criterion values and obtained criterion values are likely to differ.

With a perfect correlation (± 1.00), we can predict perfectly; the SE_{yx} will equal 0.00, for there will be no difference between predicted and obtained criterion values. With no correlation between the test and the criterion, we can assume that everyone will fall at the mean on the criterion, and we will be less wrong in doing this than we would be in making any other sort of prediction. But the SE_{yx} now will be as large as the standard deviation; let us see why.

At the left below is a formula for the standard deviation; at the right below is a formula for the standard error of estimate.

$$s_y = \sqrt{\frac{\Sigma(Y-\overline{Y})^2}{N}} \quad \text{and} \quad SE_{yx} = \sqrt{\frac{\Sigma(Y-Y')^2}{N}}, \text{where}$$

s_y = standard deviation of Y, our criterion variable

SE_{yx} = standard error of estimate (predicting values of criterion Y from known scores on Test X)

$\sqrt{}$ = "take the square root of"

Σ = "to add"

Y = obtained value on the criterion variable

$\overline{Y}$ = mean criterion value

Y' = predicted criterion value (the criterion value most likely to be associated with a specified score on Test X; determined statistically by formula)

N = number of individuals whose scores are used in the study.

The standard deviation is based on differences between obtained values and the mean $(Y - \overline{Y})$, whereas the standard error of estimate is based on differences between obtained values and predicted values $(Y - Y')$; otherwise, the formulas are identical. And, as we noted above, our best prediction is that everyone will fall at the mean when there is no correlation between test and criterion. In that event, everyone's Y' value is $\overline{Y}$, and the SE_{yx} and the standard deviation will be the same.

In other words, our predictions are no better than chance if they are based on a correlation coefficient of 0.00. Our predictions become more accurate as the correlation between test and criterion increases. And, as noted, our predictions become completely accurate when the correlation between test and criterion is ± 1.00. (Accuracy here means that obtained criterion values differ little from the predicted criterion values.)

We interpret the standard error of estimate in very much the same way we interpret a standard deviation. An illustration may be helpful:

> We know that the *Widget Winding Test* correlates positively with the number of widgets produced during a one-hour observation period. We find a SE_{yx} of 6.0 based on the correlation between WWT scores and criterion values (that is, number of widgets produced). Now we have WWT scores on 2,000 more men (who seem to be very much like those on whom the correlation was based). We want to predict how many widgets each man will produce during the one-hour observation period.
>
> Hiram Hinkley and ninety-four others earned the same WWT score, so we predict (from formulas that we can find in almost any statistics text) that all of these ninety-five men will earn the same criterion value, 44. If all of the assumptions for use of the correlation coefficient were met, and if the present group is very much like the earlier group, we will find the SE_{yx} very helpful to us. In all likelihood, the criterion values obtained by these ninety-five men will tend to be normally distributed with a mean of about 44.0 and a standard deviation of about 6.0.
>
> In the same way, eighty-eight other men have predicted criterion values of thirty-seven widgets. In all likelihood, their obtained criterion values will tend to be normally distributed with a mean of 37.0 and a standard deviation of about 6.0.
>
> If all of the assumptions are met, we may expect that there will be a normal distribution of criterion values (a separate distribution for each WWT score), that the mean of each distribution will be the

predicted criterion value, and that the standard deviation of each distribution will be given by the SE_{yx}.

But what about Hiram? It is true that his criterion value is more likely to be 44 than anything else; however, his actual obtained criterion value may be much lower or much higher. For individuals, we must expect occasional performances that differ markedly from what is predicted.

Hiram will have a criterion value that belongs in that normal distribution which has a mean of 44.0 and a standard deviation of 6.0—at least, these are the assumptions we must make. In actual fact, the assumptions are only approximated. Hiram's obtained criterion value is most likely to be 44, and the chances are approximately: two in three that it is within $\pm$ 1 SE of 44 (44 $\pm$ 6), or 38–50; ninety-five in one hundred it is within $\pm$ 2 SE of 44 (44 $\pm$ 12), or 32–56; and so on, the normal probability distribution stating the chances that Hiram's obtained criterion value will lie between any limits that we may specify.

In this way, we can set up a confidence interval for each individual's predicted criterion value. This interval represents a band of values extending out from the predicted value—a band within which the obtained criterion value has a stated probability of falling.

Standard errors of estimate (and the confidence intervals based on them) are rather large. That this is so may become more clear when we look at this next formula, another one for SE_{yx}. Though different in appearance from the one given earlier, it gives the same results.

$$SE_{yx} = s_y \sqrt{1 - r_{xy}^2} \text{, where}$$

r_{xy} = correlation coefficient between Test X and Criterion Y; i.e., a validity coefficient, and other symbols are as previously defined.

The expression, $\sqrt{1 - r_{xy}^2}$, is sometimes called the coefficient of alienation and indicates the lack of relationship between two variables. Let us take several different values of r and see what their coefficients of alienation are:

When r = 0.00, coefficient of alienation = 1.00
"   " = 0.20,   "   "   "   = 0.98
"   " = 0.40,   "   "   "   = 0.92
"   " = 0.60,   "   "   "   = 0.80
"   " = 0.866,   "   "   "   = 0.50
"   " = 1.00,   "   "   "   = 0.00

In other words, a correlation coefficient of 0.20 increases our accuracy of prediction by only 2 per cent $(1.00 - 0.98)$; an r of 0.60 only 20 per cent; and an r of 0.866 only 50 per cent. In this sense, we need an r of 0.866 to effect a 50 per cent increase in efficiency over chance.

Nevertheless, it is this coefficient of alienation that, when multiplied by the criterion's standard deviation gives us the standard error of estimate. Thus, SE_{yx} will be 0.98 as large as the standard deviation when r is 0.20; 0.80 as large when r is 0.60; 0.50 as large when r is 0.866, etc.

This seems to present a very discouraging picture. After all, we rarely get validity coefficients anywhere near as high as 0.866. We are much more likely to have validity coefficients of from about 0.20 to about 0.60—and with validity coefficients of such size, we still have a great deal of error in predicted values.

We do need very high correlations for predicting specific values with much accuracy; however, we can make general predictions very effectively with the modest-sized validities which we typically find. Consider the following example, adapted from The Psychological Corporation's *Test Service Bulletin No. 45*:

> In a given company, seventy-four stenographers were given The Psychological Corporation's *Short Employment Tests* (SET). Each stenographer was rated by a supervisor as low, average, or high in ability. The validity coefficient (based on these ratings) was just 0.38, so there would be little predictive efficiency, according to the standard error of estimate.

TABLE 2

PER CENT OF STENOGRAPHERS IN EACH THIRD ON SET-CLERICAL WHO EARNED
VARIOUS PROFICIENCY RATINGS

SET-Clerical Test Score	Proficiency Rating		
	Low	Average	High
Upper Third	18	33	50
Middle Third	29	36	28
Lowest Third	53	31	22
Total Per Cent	100	100	100
No. of Stenographers	17	39	18

*Adapted from The Psychological Corporation's *Test Service Bulletin No. 45*, "Better than Chance," (1953). (Used with permission.)

Let us see what happens if we try to predict which girls will fall into which criterion categories—instead of the specific criterion values we were concerned with in earlier examples. Table 2 shows for each criterion category the percentage of girls in each third on the Clerical part of the SET.

Wesman, author of the *Bulletin,* states, "By chance alone, the per cent of upper, middle, and low scorers in each of the rated groups would be the same—in this case, 33⅓ per cent. The boldface numbers in the table would consist of nine 33's. Note how closely this expected per cent is approximated for those ranked average in proficiency, and for those in the middle third on test score; the percentages in the middle row and those in the middle column run between 28 and 36. Note also that at the extremes—the four corner numbers—the prediction picture is more promising. Among those *rated* low, there are almost three times as many people from the lowest third on the test as there are from the top third. Among those rated high, the per cent from the top third on the test is almost two and one-half times as great as the per cent from the bottom third. The personnel man would do well to be guided by these data in selecting future stenographers, even though the validity coefficient is just 0.38."

The author of the *Bulletin* continues: "The data in the above example are based on relatively small numbers of cases (which is typically true of practical test situations) and the per cents found in each category are consequently somewhat unstable. The validity coefficients based on groups of such sizes are, of course, also less stable than coefficients based on large numbers of cases. The wise test user will make several validity studies using successive groups. Having done so, he may take an average of the validity coefficients from these studies as being a more dependable estimate of the validity of the test in his situation."

EXPECTANCY TABLES

Table 2 is an *expectancy table*—that is, a table showing the relationship between test-score intervals and criterion categories. Typically, intervals of test scores are shown at the left of the table, the number of intervals depending partly on number of cases involved and partly on the degree of differentiation desired for the situation; criterion categories are usually shown across the top of the table, the number of categories here also depending on the number of cases and on the degree of differentiation desired.

Into the individual cells of the table are placed either the number of cases or the per cent of cases which fall into that score interval and criterion category; most people prefer to use per cent, feeling that this practice is easier to interpret. Some writers feel that a picture-graph such as that shown in Table 3 is even easier to read. What high school student would not be able to understand this example? This table, too, comes from a Psychological Corporation *Test Service Bulletin* (based on a mimeographed report by Y. Y. Harris and A. A. Dole in *Research Studies in Hawaiian Education,* 1956). An expectancy table drawn in this fashion would seem to be simple enough to put into the hands of students or parents as an aid in understanding their scores; however, local policy sometimes demands that scores never be revealed to either students or parents. I believe that it is preferable for students (and others) to be given personal interpretations of their test results. When that is not feasible, however, a great deal can be accomplished by giving each student a table such as this, together with his score; even here, an effort should be made to have a counselor or teacher discuss the results with the students as a group.

Included with an expectancy table should be further information, such as: number of persons on which it is based, year when data were collected, etc. Table 3 was the result of a pilot study with 221 juniors at one Hawaiian high school who became candidates for admission to the University of Hawaii four semesters later; furthermore, it is based on only one of ten tests that were taken by these students. Multiple correlation (combining the results of several tests) would have increased accuracy of prediction, but would have been harder to explain to the students.

A similar technique, again from a Psychological Corporation *Test Service Bulletin,* is shown in Table 4. Basically, it is a bar graph—focusing our attention on those clerical workers, among sixty-five tested, who were rated as average or better by their supervisors. The number of workers involved is not very large, but there is certainly reason to believe that the company is more likely to find satisfactory clerical workers among high-scoring individuals than among lower-scoring individuals.

SUMMARY AND SUGGESTIONS   Although not too widely used in test interpretation, the expectancy table is an excellent device to use when communicating test results to laymen. It is easy to under-

TABLE 3

A Simple Expectancy Table *

What Does the Verbal Reasoning Test Tell About Academic Success at the University of Hawaii?

Of Each TEN Applicants Whose Verbal Reasoning Score Is in the	Will Not Be Accepted (KAPU)	Will Be Accepted and Will Finish the First Year With Average Grade Point Ratios of			
		0 - 1.4 Flunk Out	1.5 - 1.9 On the Edge	2.0 - 2.9 Satisfactory	3.0 & Above Exceptional
Highest Quarter (☺☺☺☺☺☺☺)		☺	☺☺	☺☺☺☺☺	☺☺☺☺
Second Quarter (☺☺☺☺☺☺☺)	☺☺	☺	☺☺	☺☺☺☺☺☺	☺
Third Quarter (☺☺☺☺☺☺☺)	☺☺	☺☺	☺☺☺	☺☺☺	
Lowest Quarter (☺☺☺☺☺☺☺)	☺☺☺☺☺☺	☺☺	☺☺	☺	

*Reprinted from The Psychological Corporation's Test Service Bulletin No. 53, "The Differential Aptitude Tests: Studies of Predictive Validity," (1958). Based on study by Y. Y. Harris and A. A. Dole in Res. Stud. in Hawaiian Educ., 1956, 1, 15 pp. mimeo. (Used with permission.)

69

TABLE 4 *

Expectancy Table and Graph Showing Per Cent Expected to Rate Average or Better in Office Clerical Tasks on the Basis of Scores on the General Clerical Test. (N = 65, Mean Score = 136.1, S.D. = 39.1, r = 31)

General Clerical Test Scores	No. in score group	No. rated average or better	% rated average or better						
200-up	5	5	100						
150-199	18	15	83						
100-149	31	23	74						
50-99	11	6	55						
Total	65			0%	20%	40%	60%	80%	100%

*Reprinted from The Psychological Corporation's *Test Service Bulletin No. 38*, "Expectancy Tables," (1949). (Used with permission.)

stand and to explain to others. It directs attention to the purpose of testing by comparing test scores with criterion performance.

Furthermore, the expectancy table is an aid in test interpretation that shows a realistic outlook so far as criterion results are concerned. A common misinterpretation of test scores goes something like this: "This score means that you will fail in college." No test score (except, perhaps, a final examination in some course!) means any such thing. The expectancy table encourages an interpretation of this sort: "In the past, students with scores like yours have seldom succeeded at our college; in fact, only two students in ten have had satisfactory averages at the end of their first year." This latter type of interpretation can be supported; the former cannot.

When interpreting the results of an expectancy table, we should keep these points in mind:

1. We need to be certain that we are using the same test (including same form, level, edition, etc.).
2. The table is based on results that have been found in the past; it may or may not be relevant to the present group (or individual).
3. If the table is based on the performance of people from another office (company, school, or college), it may or may not apply to ours.
4. We can have more confidence in expectancy tables which are

based on large numbers of scores. (Percentages are sometimes used to disguise small numbers.)

5. Even with no special training in testing or statistics, we can make expectancy tables of our own very easily. (Several issues of the Psychological Corporation's *Test Service Bulletin* contain excellent suggestions written by Alexander G. Wesman; see especially *Bulletin No. 38.*)

6. An expectancy table may be used to spot individuals (or subgroups) that do not perform as we would expect; by noting instances in which predictions miss, we may check back to discover possible reasons for the failure.

7. In a sense we may think of an expectancy table as a set of norms in which one's test score is compared with the criterion performance of others who have made that same score.

AN OMISSION AND AN EXPLANATION

Some readers will be surprised that I chose to terminate the discussion of inferential statistics without mentioning many of the most important such statistics. There are many more inferential statistics that a well-trained test user should know if he is to read the testing literature or conduct research with tests. He should know that there are standard errors of differences, for example, and he should know that there are statistical tests of significance, etc. But these are topics which are not essential to an understanding of psychological and educational test scores, and I have chosen to omit them for that reason.

Other readers (or perhaps the same ones) will be surprised that I included expectancy tables in this chapter on statistics. Does it not belong in the chapter on norms or, perhaps, the one on types of derived scores? Certainly the topic might have been located in either of those chapters; perhaps it should have a chapter all its own. I added the topic to this chapter because I felt that the logical basis for expectancy tables was developed naturally from the discussion of the standard error of estimate. I hope that my readers agree that the transition was easily accomplished.

Chapter Five ## NORMS

Two graduate students, Susie and Tom, were discussing *raw scores*. "Why, they don't mean a thing!" Susie said.

"You're crazy!" said Tom. "They're the most important kind of score there is."

They are both right. If raw scores are not accurate, nothing else can be. Yet, in themselves, raw scores mean very little.

Una Uhrbrock has a score of 79. What does 79 mean? If it is a raw score, it probably means that Una answered seventy-nine test items correctly. But is that good or bad? High or low? Above average or below? We cannot say without more information.

If we know how many items there were on the test, we can translate the raw score into a percentage correct score. This gives us a little better understanding of Una's performance, but only in an absolute sense; we know her performance as some percentage of a perfect score, but that is all.

Still more information is needed before we can approach any complete understanding of that 79. Specifically, we need information about scores which have been obtained by other people and we need a description of what these other people are like.

In short, we need a set of norms to understand how well Una did or what is meant by her score of 79. *Norms* are the results obtained by a specified group on a specified test. Norms provide a standard against which we may compare any given raw score value. (Some writers object to using the word, *standard*. The objection is valid only if standard is used to imply a level of quality that should be obtained by everyone. As we have used the term, *standard* implies only a set of results which may be used for meaningful comparisons.)

When I was a child, my grandmother used to mark my height on the inside of a door frame every six months or so. Other pencil marks indicated the heights of my father, my brother, and others— all of them also dutifully recorded at intervals of about six months throughout their childhoods. My grandmother used these marks as a standard for gauging my growth. We may criticize the randomness and size of her sample, but these records constituted a crude set of norms—that is, a set of standards for comparing my height at specified ages with the heights of others.

We may set up standards of quality for any purpose or situation; however, quality standards and norms are not synonymous and should not be confused. As, for example:

Paul Petry made the lowest score in the fifth grade at the Executive Heights School on a recent reading comprehension test. He was well below his class norm and slightly below the national norm for children of his age. The fact that Paul is somewhat below average in this important ability does not mean that he should be failed; it does mean that Paul did less well than others with whom he is being compared. His teacher must decide whether Paul's work is so poor that he should be failed. The fact that he was below average on this test should not be the basis for his failure.

It is a sad, but inescapable, fact that about one-half of any group is below average. The very definition of *average* demands it. Paul is only one of thousands upon thousands of youngsters throughout the country whose performance on this test has been below average. We cannot get away from it: the average for any group demands that there be values below as well as above it.

But the nature of the *norms* (comparison) *group* is extremely important. Paul had the lowest score of all of the fifth-graders in his school; however, he may have done far better than most fifth-graders in the Bottoms District School. We must always consider the nature of the normative group. It can make a considerable difference.

THE NORM

The simplest statement of norms is given by *the norm*. This is nothing more than the average (either mean or median) score for a specified group. Norm is used occasionally as a synonym for average, as in the example of Paul Petry.

A norm is also used sometimes in place of more complete norms if the available scores are inadequate, inappropriate, or suspect for some reason. On a new test, for example, scores may be available on very few people or the people who have been tested may be too heterogeneous to be considered as a norms group. In such instances, it may be better to describe a person's performance merely as being above or below the norm for those tested to date.

A third general use for the norm is found in situations where the test publisher wishes to report averages for a number of groups (each perhaps involving only a few examinees) or the averages of a single group on several tests. Research workers make similar use of the norm in summarizing results and in showing trends for several groups.

TYPES OF NORMS

A set of norms for a test consists of a table giving corresponding values of raw scores and derived scores. Derived scores are intended to make test interpretation easier and more meaningful than is possible with raw scores alone.

Derived Scores

Norms are frequently designated according to the type of score involved; we may, for example, read of percentile norms, grade-equivalent norms, etc. Because of the large number of different types of derived score in common use, we are devoting one entire chapter (Chapter Six) to discussing them. In the present chapter we shall see several examples of norms tables, but will have no detailed discussion of the scores.

Norms Tables

A good norms table should include a derived-score equivalent for each raw score that can be made. It should include a full description of the group on which it is based. It may present one or several types of derived score for one or several groups.

When a norms table is incomplete, it may be confusing to the test user.

I once gave a wide variety of individual and group tests to a coed of unusually high ability. One of many tests on which she excelled was a test, still in its experimental form, which I had never given before. I scored it carefully and found a raw score of 34. The maximum possible score seemed to be 36, but the norms table went up only to 27. I spent several hours in reviewing the scoring instructions and all related information. Finally, months later, I questioned the test's author. His reply? "I thought that 27 was high enough. Almost no one gets a score as high as that."

Simple Norms Table

The simplest norms tables consist of two columns, one containing raw-score values and the other containing corresponding derived-score values. Table 5 illustrates such a table with hypothetical re-

TABLE 5

EXAMPLE OF SIMPLE NORMS TABLE

Percentile Norms for the Hypothetical *Technician's Aptitude and Proficiency Test**

Raw Score	Percentile	Raw Score	Percentile	Raw Score	Percentile	Raw Score	Percentile
11	98	8	75	5	34	2	10
10	96	7	62	4	23	1	4
9	85	6	48	3	18	0	1

*Hypothetical data. Presumably based on 6245 laboratory technicians tested during the past year at 450 hospital laboratories and 785 industrial and commercial laboratories in 39 states. [The complete list of participating laboratories should be included in the manual or made available upon request.]

sults presumed to be based on a national sample of laboratory technicians. Note that the group is described in some detail. The test manual should list the laboratories which contributed data (or should make the list available on request). In this present example, we might still ask questions about the educational background and work experience of the examinees, for these factors could influence our interpretation.

In Table 5, we might interpret a raw score of 6 in this manner: *This person scored as high as or higher than 48 per cent of the national sample of laboratory technicians used as the normative sample.* Note, however, that with so short a test we would need to be very cautious in interpreting any individual score; therefore, we might prefer to say merely that this person scored *about average when compared with national norms.*

Multiple-Group Norms Table

Very often a norms table is constructed to show results from several groups in a single table. Besides the obvious economy in printing, this practice permits us to compare a person's raw score with as many of these groups as we wish. Table 6 illustrates such a table with data drawn from Project TALENT, and is based on a 4 per cent random sample of the approximately 440,000 high school students tested in 1960 as part of that research study. The test we are concerned with is the *Information Test–Aeronautics and Space.* Here again there are so few items that we must be cautious in interpreting individual scores. The chance passing of one more item or chance failing of one more item would make a great apparent difference in performance.

> Pauline, a ninth-grade girl, had a score of 3; this gives her a percentile rank of 65 when compared with other ninth-grade girls. Pauline knows very little about aeronautics and space, and she might easily have missed one more item; that would have placed her at the fortieth percentile. On the other hand, if she had happened to guess correctly on one or two more items than she did, she would have had a percentile rank of 83 or 93.

With very short tests such as this, reliability is likely to be extremely low—especially when the items are so difficult that lucky guessing becomes important in determining one's score. We should be very careful in making any interpretations of individual test scores here except for students clearly at one extreme or the other.

We can rely on group differences to a far greater extent. Note that there is no level at which girls have done better than boys, nor is there any level at which youngsters in one grade have done better than those in any higher grade. As we have noted before we often can have confidence in group differences in test performance even

TABLE 6

Example of Multiple-Group Norms Table

Percentile Norms for the *Information Test-Aeronautics and Space*, of the Project TALENT Test Battery*

Raw Score	Percentile Score							
	Grade 9		Grade 10		Grade 11		Grade 12	
	Boy	Girl	Boy	Girl	Boy	Girl	Boy	Girl
10	99+	99+	99	99+	99	99+	98	99+
9	97	99+	96	99+	96	99+	92	99
8	92	99+	91	99+	89	99+	84	99
7	86	99	83	99	80	99	75	98
6	78	97	73	96	69	96	63	95
5	66	93	62	92	55	91	51	89
4	52	83	47	81	41	79	36	77
3	36	65	31	62	26	61	22	59
2	20	40	16	40	14	38	11	38
1	8	18	6	18	5	16	4	16
0	2	4	1	4	1	4	1	3

*Based on a 4% random sample of the approximately 440,000 high school students in 50 states tested in 1960 as part of the Project TALENT study directed by John C. Flanagan. Reprinted from *Project TALENT Counselors' Technical Manual for Interpreting Test Scores,* 1961, University of Pittsburgh. (Used with permission.)

when test reliability is too low to permit much confidence in individual scores.

> Note that a raw score of 4 has a percentile rank of 83 on ninth-grade girls' norms, but of only 36 on twelfth-grade boys' norms. A twelfth-grade boy would have to answer twice as many items correctly in order to have a percentile rank as high as that given to a ninth-grade girl for a score of 4.

Multiple-Score Norms Table

Sometimes a norms table includes derived scores for each of several tests (or subtests). For obvious reasons this should never be done unless the same norms group is used for each test. Sometimes scaled scores (*see* Chapter Six) are used instead of raw scores, especially when some of the subtests have many more items than do others. An example is Table 7, showing percentile ranks for second-semester high school juniors on the *National Merit Scholarship Qualifying Test*.

To make full use of this table in a practical situation, we would need to know and understand the nature of NMSQT standard scores and how they were made comparable to scores on the *Iowa Tests of Educational Development*. These points are explained in the technical report from which this table was taken. We are using the table only as an illustration and have omitted part of it in order to save space.

Abbreviated Norms Tables

An occasional norms table includes only alternate raw-score values (or, perhaps, every fifth raw-score value), thereby forcing the test user to interpolate whenever he has a nontabled raw score. Such a table saves money in printing, but it encourages mistakes and costs the test user additional time and trouble. Abbreviated tables used to be common, but are becoming increasingly rare.

Condensed Norms Tables

Very similar to the abbreviated table is the condensed table, where selected percentile values are given and the corresponding

TABLE 7

EXAMPLE OF A MULTIPLE-SCORE NORMS TABLE

National *Iowa Tests of Educational Development* Percentiles for the
National Merit Scholarship Qualifying Test Scores for Second-Semester
High School Juniors*

NMSQT Standard Scores	1 English Usage	2 Math. Usage	3 Soc. Studies Reading	4 Nat. Sci. Reading	5 Word Usage	Composite Score	NMSQT Standard Scores
36							36
35							35
34							34
33							33
32							32
31							31
30		99		99			30
29		98	99	98	99		29
28		98	98	97	98	99	28
27	99	97	97	96	97	98	27
26	98	97	95	95	96	97	26
25	96	95	93	93	93	96	25
24	94	94	91	90	90	94	24
23	91	92	88	87	87	92	23
.	.	.	.	.	.	.	.
.	.	.	.	.	.	.	.
.	.	.	.	.	.	.	.
11	16	34	24	27	21	21	11
10	12	26	19	22	16	16	10
9	9	21	15	17	12	12	9
8	7	17	11	13	9	8	8
7	4	14	7	9	7	5	7
6	3	11	4	7	5	3	6
5	2	9	2	5	3	2	5
4	1	7	2	4	2	1	4
3		5	1	3	1		3
2		3	1	2			2
1		1	1	1			1
0		1	1				0

*Estimated *ITED* percentiles of the 1960 *NMSQT* scores. Basis for determining equivalent scores accompanies the complete table, which appears in *National Merit Scholarship Qualifying Test Spring 1960 Technical Report,* 1960, Science Research Associates, Chicago. (Used with permission.)

raw scores shown. This style of table is still used occasionally, but not so often for general use today as in the past. Such tables are used often for illustrative data when there are few people in a group (and the publisher is reluctant to present complete norms for that reason), or when the publisher wishes to present a large amount of data in a single table for comparison purposes.

Table 8 illustrates condensed national percentile norms for the first four of the *Flanagan Aptitude Classification Tests* (FACT). The original table contained similar information for the remaining fifteen tests—all on a single page. Note that the entries in this table are the raw scores; since only selected percentiles are to be shown, the usual positions of raw and derived scores are reversed.

TABLE 8

EXAMPLE OF A CONDENSED NORMS TABLE

Condensed National Percentile Norms for Four of the
*Flanagan Aptitude Classification Tests**

| | | | | | Percentiles | | | | Maximum Possible |
Test	Grade	1	10	25	50	75	90	99	Raw Score
1 Inspection	9	16	30	35	42	49	56	73	80
	10	17	30	37	44	52	61	77	80
	11	19	33	39	47	55	64	79	80
	12	21	34	41	49	57	64	79	80
	9	3	5	7	9	11	14	20	30
2 Mechanics	10	3	6	8	10	12	15	22	30
	11	4	6	8	10	13	16	23	30
	12	4	6	8	11	14	19	25	30
	9	6	19	28	37	46	55	73	120
3 Tables	10	6	21	30	41	50	60	86	120
	11	6	23	33	44	55	65	93	120
	12	7	25	36	48	59	70	97	120
	9	1	3	4	6	9	12	18	24
4 Reasoning	10	1	3	5	7	10	13	18	24
	11	1	3	5	8	12	15	18	24
	12	1	4	6	9	13	17	22	24

*Condensed norms for all 19 tests in the *FACT* battery are given in the original single-page table in John C. Flanagan's *FACT Technical Report*, 1959, Science Research Associates. (Used here with permission.)

At this point we need to mention expectancy tables and charts once again. (*See* pages 66-71 for a more complete discussion.) They differ from norms tables in one important characteristic: whereas norms tables state derived-score values corresponding to each raw score, expectancy tables show criterion performance for each interval of raw scores. In all other respects, expectancy tables are the same as norms tables. We might re-emphasize here that expectancy tables, like norms tables, state the results found for some specified group. When interpreting anyone's score through the use of either an expectancy table or norms table, we must consider whether the group and the situation are comparable.

Articulation of Norms

A specified test may vary in edition, form, and/or level. *Edition* refers usually to date of publication (1963 edition, etc.). Different editions may be needed to keep test content up to date.

Form refers usually to an equivalent version; that is, different forms will contain different items, but will be similar in content and difficulty. Different forms may be needed to insure test security; i.e., to minimize the likelihood of test items leaking out to examinees. Different form designations may also be given when item content is identical, but scoring method is different; for example, Form AH may be designed for hand-scoring and Form AM for machine-scoring.

Level refers usually to the age or grade placement of those for whom a specified version of the test is intended. Different levels may be needed to make subject content and item difficulty appropriate for the examinees; from three to eight levels sometimes are used to cover the range of school grades.

Some excellent tests exist in only a single edition, form, and level. The need for multiple versions of a test becomes greater as the test is used more widely. Thus, the need is greatest, especially for different levels, with tests designed for wide-scale administration throughout whole school systems.

New editions are intended, with few exceptions, to replace and to improve upon earlier editions. There may or may not be a desire to make results from two editions directly comparable. Nearly always, however, it is important to make different forms and levels yield comparable results; the aim is to achieve articulated (neatly jointed) norms.

All major publishers of tests for schools are aware of this need for articulation and all take steps toward insuring comparability. The exact procedures followed differ, and some publishers are more successful than others. All are more successful in attaining comparability of their own respective products than they are in achieving comparability with each other's products.

Those of us who use tests should check the evidence of articulation studies to see how comparable the results from different forms and levels should be. This information should be found in a test manual or technical supplement under such headings as Articulation, Interlocking Studies, Overlapping Norms, and the like. Unfortunately it is more difficult to obtain information about the comparability of tests from different publishers, and this is likely to continue to be true until publishers can agree upon a single large nationally representative sample which may be used as a common reference group. There is some reason to believe that the Project TALENT study (directed by John C. Flanagan of the University of Pittsburgh) may supply this need for anchoring norms.

NORMS GROUPS

We cannot emphasize too much the tremendous importance of the norms group. Regardless of the type of norms, we are dealing with results that are based on some group of people. But it makes a great deal of difference *which* group of people. Consider the example of Arthur Amrine:

> Arthur Amrine, a graduate assistant in philosophy at Athol University, answered 210 words correctly on a vocabulary test of 300 items. His raw score of 210 means that he did as well as or better than:
> 99% of the seventh grade pupils in Athol
> 92% of the Athol High School seniors
> 91% of the high school graduates in Jones, Ohio
> 85% of the entering freshmen at Edie College
> 70% of the philosophy majors at Athol University

55% of the graduating seniors at Athol University
40% of the graduate assistants at Athol University
15% of the English professors at Athol University
Although Arthur's absolute performance (210 words defined correctly) remains unchanged, our impression of how well he has done
may differ markedly as we change norms groups.

This illustration is extreme. Under no normal circumstances
would we compare a graduate assistant's score with those of
seventh-grade pupils; however, results every bit as far-fetched as
these can be obtained in real-life situations—and results nearly as
far-fetched often do occur.

Even professional measurements people occasionally are fooled
by differences in norms groups, as in the following situation:

Two tests (scholastic aptitude and reading comprehension) put
out by the same, highly reputable publisher, often have been used
together in college admissions batteries. At most colleges students
have tended to stand relatively higher on the scholastic aptitude test
than on the reading comprehension test. The norms most commonly
used have been the national norms prepared by the publisher and
based on thousands of cases from colleges in all sections of the country. The norms could be trusted. Or could they?

The norms should not have been accepted as readily as they
were, because a more select group of colleges unintentionally was
used in establishing the reading test norms. The net result has been
that most students who take both tests seem to do more poorly in
reading comprehension than in scholastic aptitude.

Before this difference in norms groups was generally recognized,
interoffice memoranda were exchanged at many colleges—asking
why their students were so deficient in reading ability!

This same sort of difficulty is encountered frequently in school
testing—especially when we use tests from different publishers.

Acme Test Company has used a sample of 5,000 students from
forty schools in twenty-four states in standardizing its *Acme Achievement Battery* (AAB) for the fourth, fifth, and sixth grades. Several
rather select schools were included, but no below-average ones.
Better Tests, Inc. used about 4,500 students from thirty-five schools
in twenty states in standardizing its *Better Achievement Battery*
(BAB) for the same grades; however, their researchers were more
careful in the selection of schools and obtained a more representative national sample of these grades.

Let us assume that both batteries were very carefully developed
and that they are very similar in content and item difficulty. Pupils
still will tend to receive lower scores on the AAB than on the BAB.

The following situation shows what may often happen in real-life school settings where different achievement batteries are used at different grade levels.

> Miss Smith's pupils are tested on the AAB at the end of the fifth grade; their mean grade-placement score is 5.4 (which is about one-half grade below the expected norm for her class). These same pupils had taken the BAB at the end of the fourth grade and had earned a mean grade-placement score of 5.0 (very slightly above the norm at that time). It looks as if Miss Smith has not taught much to her class, especially when these pupils take the BAB again at the end of their sixth grade and obtain a mean grade-placement score of 7.1 (once again slightly above the norm for their actual grade-placement).
>
> Miss Smith is a victim of circumstances. If her pupils had taken the AAB at the end of the fourth grade and had taken the BAB at the end of the fifth grade, her pupils would have shown great apparent improvement during their year with her.

This same sort of thing happens in industrial settings where test-naïve personnel workers fail to consider the differences in norms groups from test to test. "After all," they may reason, "Test Y and Test Z were both standardized on mechanical employees." And such personnel workers may ignore the fact that the mechanical employees used for the Test Y norms were engineering technicians whereas those used for Test Z were machine-wipers and machine-cleaners.

The list of possible mistaken inferences could be extended almost indefinitely. The point we must remember is: be sure to understand the nature of the norms groups. And understand it in as much detail as the publisher will permit through his descriptions.

Which Norms to Use

Most test manuals include several norms tables. Which should we use? The obvious general answer is that we should use whichever norms are most appropriate for the individual examinee and the situation involved.

We seldom have much difficulty in selecting an appropriate set of norms to use when the test is a maximum-performance test designed for routine school use. With tests not commonly given to all pupils in a school (for example, specific aptitude tests) or tests designed primarily for out-of-school use, our selection is likely to be much more difficult. For a clerical aptitude test, we may have to decide whether an examinee should be compared with 225 female clerk-typists employed by a large insurance company, 456 female applicants for clerical positions with four midwestern companies, or 839 female eleventh-grade students in a secretarial sequence. This same problem exists with many (if not most) tests.

In guidance situations we often decide to use several different norms groups:

> Dottie Divenger has taken an art aptitude test. Her score would place her very high among nonart students and adults, high average among first-year students at an art academy, and low average among employed fashion designers. All of this information may be helpful to Dottie in deciding whether to enter a career in art, whether to attend an art academy, etc.

There are even occasions when we may deliberately employ norms which appear to be unsuitable. In counseling a young lady interested in a predominantly male occupation, I would compare her scores with male norms as well as female norms. She is, after all, contemplating a career in direct competition with men and she should be compared with them.

Local Norms

Local norms are sometimes better than *national norms*. Developing our own norms is not too difficult. We keep a careful record of the test scores made by a defined group (all applicants for some sort of position; all bookkeepers currently employed by our company; all fourth-grade pupils in our school district, etc.) until a satisfactory number have been acquired. We arrange the scores in a frequency distribution and assign appropriate derived scores (*see* Chapter Six).

I have used the term local norms here to mean any set of norms developed by the test user; by national norms, I mean those developed and made available by the test publisher.

Circumstances help us to decide whether we should be satisfied with available national norms or whether we should develop our own. In the first place, we have no choice unless we are using the same test on a large number of people. If we use a particular test only once in a while, we will have to depend on national norms because we will not have enough of our own scores to do much good.

If national norms are suitable, we have no problem. We can use them without difficulty if we want to.

Even when the national norms are not especially appropriate, we may prefer to use them rather than to develop our own—as when it seems that nothing is to be gained by developing our own. On an interest test used for guidance purposes, for example, we may have very little to gain by comparing an individual's score with other local scores.

On the other hand, even though there are adequate national norms, there may be situations in which we would like to be able to compare individuals with other local people. We may be much more interested in knowing how well an applicant compares with other local applicants than in knowing how well he has done when compared with some national normative group.

ASSORTED TESTS AND INTEGRATED BATTERIES

Tremendous strides have been made in psychological and educational testing during recent years. After all, the entire testing movement is not very old. Binet and Simon gave us the first intelligence test in 1905. The first group intelligence test and the first personality inventory appeared during World War I. With the exception of a few standardized achievement test batteries which first came out during the late 1920's and 1930's, almost all tests published prior to World War II were separate tests. By this I mean that each new test was developed independently of every other, and very little effort was made to equate norms groups.

Inevitably the test user would find himself with results which looked like these (hypothetical, of course) for Judy Jessel:

PR of 96 on reading speed; compared with high school students
PR of 77 on reading comprehension; compared with college freshmen
IQ of 109 on an intelligence test
IQ of 131 on another intelligence test
Standard score of 59 on clerical aptitude; compared with clerks
Score of B+ on mechanical aptitude; female norms.

Under such conditions, even skilled counselors had difficulty making much sense from the results. As each test had been developed independently by a different author, usually to meet some important need, no one could safely compare the score on one test with the score on another.

The situation has been improving rapidly since World War II. Nearly all of the major publishers now have at least one multiple-aptitude test battery in which all of the tests have been standardized on the same group and the norms for which are all based on the same group. With integrated batteries such as these, we can now begin to make comparisons of various scores made by the same person. Has Judy done better on clerical aptitude than on reading comprehension, better on reading speed than on mechanical aptitude? The use of tests in guidance demands answers to such questions, and with integrated test batteries we can begin to find these answers. Some difficulties, however, do remain (*see* Chapter Seven).

There are still many assorted tests which are not part of any integrated test battery. There probably always will be. If we are concerned with selecting people (whether for employment or for training), we want to use the test (or tests) which will do the best job for us; there is no reason why we should consider whether or not a test is part of an integrated battery. An integrated battery of tests is most important in guidance and in differential placement, where the common norms group is valuable in making comparisons of a person's relative ability within the various test areas.

SOME BASIC RULES

Here are some basic rules to follow in using norms:

1. Study the norms supplied by the publisher, paying particular attention to the description of the normative groups.
2. Study the articulation research if different forms and/or levels of a test have been used.
3. Select the norms group (or groups) most appropriate for the examinee and the situation.
4. Norms groups which sound similar may or may not be similar. Never *assume* that two norms groups are similar.
5. Never make direct comparisons of a person's scores on two or

more tests unless the scores are based on the same norms groups.

6. Develop local norms if none of the publisher's norms is adequate or if frequent comparisons are to be made of scores from tests not within the same integrated battery.
7. Check the type of score being used. Understand it completely.
8. Study the norms table. Try interpreting a given raw score—does it make sense?
9. Think! Use common sense!
10. Check the results!

Chapter Six # DERIVED SCORES

As noted in the last chapter, we need accurate raw scores so that we can have accurate derived scores. No amount of statistical manipulation can compensate for using a poor test or for mistakes in giving or scoring any test. Nor can the use of derived scores reduce measurement error or increase precision in prediction.

There are two main purposes for using derived scores: (1) to make scores from different tests comparable by expressing them on the same scale, and/or (2) to make possible more meaningful interpretations of scores. We will find that there are many derived scores, each having its own advantages and limitations.

A CLASSIFICATION SCHEME

The following outline is intended for classifying types of derived score used in reporting maximum-performance tests. With minor modifications the outline would be suitable for typical-performance tests as well, but they are not our concern.

The score a person receives on any maximum-performance test depends in part upon his knowledge and skill and upon his motivation while taking the test. These elements play their part in determining a person's score, regardless of how the score is expressed; they are, in fact, the kinds of things we are trying to measure when we give the tests. Beyond these common elements, we shall find three principal bases for expressing test scores: (1) comparison with an "absolute standard," or content difficulty; (2) interindividual comparison, and (3) intra-individual comparison. My classification scheme centers about these four major categories:

I. Comparison with an "Absolute Standard"; or Content Difficulty

    A. Percentage correct scores
    B. Letter grades (sometimes)

II. Interindividual Comparison

    A. Considering mean and standard deviation of the group (linear standard scores)
        1. z-scores
        2. T-scores
        3. $AGCT$-scores
        4. $CEEB$-scores
        5. Deviation IQ's (sometimes)
            (a) Wechsler IQ's
            (b) Stanford-Binet IQ's

    B. Considering rank within groups
        1. Ranks
        2. Percentile ranks and percentile bands
        3. Letter grades (sometimes)
        4. Normalized standard scores (area transformations)
            (a) T-scaled scores
            (b) Stanine scores
            (c) C-scaled scores
            (d) Sten scores
            (e) Deviation IQ's (sometimes)
                (1) Wechsler subtests
            (f) $ITED$-scores
        5. Decile ranks

    C. Considering the range of scores in a group
        1. Percent placement

D. Considering status of those obtaining same score
 1. Age scores
   (a) Mental ages
   (b) Educational ages, etc.
 2. Grade-placement scores
   (a) Full-population grade-placement
   (b) Modal-age grade-placement
   (c) Modal-age and modal-intelligence grade-placement
   (d) Anticipated-achievement grade-placement
   (e) Mental-age grade-placement

III. Intra-Individual Comparison (of two measures of the individual)
 A. Ratio IQ's
 B. Intellectual Status Index
 C. Educational Quotients
 D. Accomplishment Quotients

IV. Assorted Arbitrary Bases
 A. Nonmeaningful scaled scores
 B. Long-range equi-unit scales
 C. Deviation IQ's (Otis-style)

In a normal distribution (*see* Chapter Four), most of these derived scores are interrelated. As shown in Figure 10 of Chart 2, we can make transformations from one kind of score to another very easily if we assume a normal distribution based on the same group of individuals. Under these two assumptions, *normality* and *same group*, the relationships shown in Figure 10 will always exist. When different groups are involved, we cannot make direct comparisons; when the set of scores cannot be assumed to be distributed normally, we find that some of the relationships are changed while others still hold.

A certain test has been given locally and is found to have a mean of 300 and a standard deviation of 40. When we notice that the distribution of scores seems to resemble closely the normal probability distribution, and we are willing to treat our set of scores as being normal, what can we say about the scores? Let us take a couple of cases and see.

Bob has a raw score of 300. This would give him a z-score of 0.00, a T-score of 50, a stanine of 5, a percentile rank of 50, etc.

Patricia has a raw score of 320. This would give her a z-score of 0.5, a T-score of 55, a stanine of 6, a percentile rank of 69, etc.

Figure 10 has been drawn with a number of additional baselines. Each of these can be used equally well as the graph's abscissa. To change from one type of score to another, we merely move vertically to another line.

Figure 11 of Chart 2 shows some of these same types of score in a badly skewed distribution. The sole purpose of this figure is to indicate those scores which change in their relationship to others. Somewhat less detail has been shown here, for this distribution is not subject to generalization as was the distribution in Figure 10. Note that z- and T-scores do not change in their relationship to each other, nor would their relationship to raw scores change. Normalized standard scores and percentiles maintain a constant relationship between each other—but they do not relate to z- and T-scores (nor to raw scores) in the same manner as in the normal distribution.

Discussion of the Classification Scheme

Type I scores are probably the most familiar, for they are commonly used in reporting the results of classroom tests. These scores are unique in that they consider only the specified individual's performance; the performance of all other examinees is ignored in assigning the score. In a sense Type I scores compare each examinee individually with an absolute standard of perfection (as represented by a perfect score on the test). This absolute-standard reasoning has an attractive appeal at first glance; however, thoughtful testers soon realize that the individual's score may depend more on the difficulty of the tasks presented by the test items than on the individual's ability. Type I scores are not suited for use with standardized tests (although letter grades based on interindividual comparison are sometimes used with such tests). When test scores are based on each person's own absolute level of performance, we have no way of illustrating the scores in a generalized fashion. (In other words, the mean and standard deviation are likely to differ for each test— and we have no typical distribution to illustrate.)

With *Type II A* scores, we can show how scores are likely to be distributed for any group. Type II A scores are known as linear standard scores and they will always reflect the original distribution of raw scores; that is, if we were to draw separate graphs of the

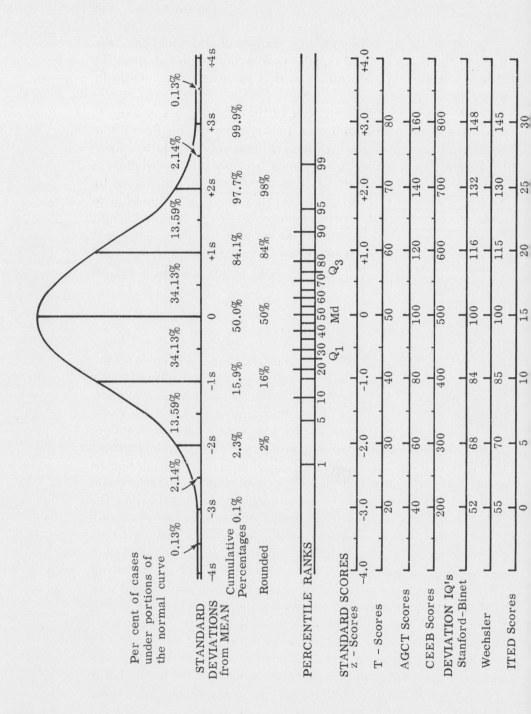

Per cent of cases
under portions of
the normal curve

STANDARD
DEVIATIONS from MEAN

Cumulative Percentages

Rounded

PERCENTILE RANKS

STANDARD SCORES
z – Scores

T – Scores

AGCT Scores

CEEB Scores

DEVIATION IQ's
Stanford-Binet

Wechsler

ITED Scores

STANINES	1	2	3	4	5	6	7	8	9
Per cent in stanine	4%	7%	12%	17%	20%	17%	12%	7%	4%

C-SCORES	0	1	2	3	4	5	6	7	8	9	10
Per cent in C-Scores	1%	3%	7%	12%	17%	20%	17%	12%	7%	3%	1%

STEN	1	2	3	4	5	6	7	8	9	10
Per cent in sten	2%	5%	9%	15%	19%	19%	15%	9%	5%	2%

Figure 10.

STANDARD DEVIATIONS from MEAN	-2s	-1s	0	+1s	+2s	+3s	+4s
PERCENTILE RANKS	1	25	50	75	99		
T - Score	30	40	50	60	70	80	90
T - Scaled Score	27	43	50	57		73	

CHART 2

Relationships of Selected Scores in a Normal Distribution (Figure 10) and in a Positively Skewed Distribution (Figure 11)

Figure 11.

95

distributions of raw scores and of their standard-score equivalents, the two graphs would have identical shapes—and we can change with accuracy from raw scores to standard scores and back again.

With *Type II B* scores, we lose information about the shape of the distribution of raw scores unless the original distribution was normal (and of course it can never be perfectly normal). With nonnormal distributions we lose information that would be necessary to re-create the shape of the raw-score distribution; for example, when we use ranks, we lose all information as to how far apart the scores of any two examinees are. Even with Type II B scores, however, we can generalize the score systems to show what relationships always exist within a normal distribution.

Type II C is a special case. If the distribution of raw scores were normal, we could show the relationship of per cent placement scores to other types of score—except for one thing: per cent placement is based on the range between the two most extreme scores, and the normal curve ranges from values of $+\infty$ to $-\infty$.

With *Type II D* scores, the values expressed are averages of groups which differ in age or in grade placement. It would be impossible to generalize these scores, for they are specific to each test and group.

Type III scores are based on intra-individual comparisons and there is no reason to expect that such scores could be generalized; therefore, we cannot show how such scores would be distributed except for a specified test and group.

Type IV scores are an assortment which does not fit readily into this classification scheme. They are primarily scaled scores with more or less arbitrary values and not intended for interpretation in themselves.

Comparison of Type II A and Type II B Scores

As we noted in the previous section, it is possible to generalize Type II A and (to some extent) Type II B scores. In other words, we can show graphically how these scores relate to each other. If the original distribution of raw scores were perfectly normal, we would find the scores related as shown in Figure 10 and we could translate freely from one type of score to the next.

Whenever we interpret scores of either Type II A or Type II B, we may find it convenient to assume that the scores for the norm group were normally distributed. In fact, normalized standard scores (Type II B 4) are designed specifically to yield a distribution that is essentially normal even if the distribution of raw scores is far from normal.

Paired with Figure 10 in Chart 2 is Figure 11, a badly skewed distribution. Figure 11 is a specific departure from the normal probability model and is not generalizable. Other distributions might be more (or less) skewed in the same direction, skewed in the other direction, truncated, bimodal, multimodal, etc. The sole purpose of including Figure 11 is to show which relationships remain the same and which change when the distribution of original scores differs from normal.

Another aid to understanding the similarities and differences among these scores is to be found in Table 10 in the Appendix. It is a concise tabular arrangement of all derived scores mentioned in this chapter and, whenever appropriate, contains for each type of score: formula, basic rationale, advantages, limitations, and illustrative score values.

A still further aid to understanding Type II A and Type II B scores is Table 9 in the Appendix. This table shows comparable values of several commonly used derived-score systems which exist within a normal distribution; it presents in tabular form the same information contained in Figure 10.

THE SCORES

In discussing these scores, we are assuming at least a basic understanding of: the mean, median, standard deviation, range, and the normal probability curve. These concepts, developed in Chapter Four, should be reviewed by the reader who feels uncertain of them at this point.

We shall use the same order here as was used in the outline on pages 91 and 92. After a brief introductory section stating the general characteristics of scores of a given type, we shall consider for each specific score: the use, characteristics and rationale, an illustrative example, and the advantages and limitations. A brief summary will also be given for a few of the more important scores.

TYPE I: COMPARISON WITH AN ABSOLUTE STANDARD, OR CONTENT DIFFICULTY

These scores are suited only for maximum-performance tests and are rarely used except as scores on classroom achievement tests. As noted earlier in the chapter, one's performance on any maximum-performance test is determined in part by his knowledge and skill and by his motivation; these elements are common in determining any person's level of performance. The only other important determinant of any person's Type I score is the difficulty of the test content, for the person's performance is being compared with perfection (that is, with the maximum-possible score on the test). The scores of other examinees play no part in determining the score of any specified examinee.

Type I A. Percentage Correct

The *percentage correct* score is used in reporting the results of classroom achievement tests, but is almost never used with any other type of test. As noted above, it compares an examinee's score with the maximum-possible score. Viewed differently, it may be thought of as one's score per 100 items. In either case, the resulting percentage correct score is the same.

FORMULA:

$X_{\%c} = 100R/T$, where
$X_{\%c}$ = per cent correct score
R = number of right answers (items answered correctly)
T = total number of items on test.

EXAMPLE:

Horace Head answers correctly forty-four items on a fifty-item test. His percentage correct score is 88. $[(100 \times 44)/50 = 88]$.

Percentage correct scores are the only derived scores (except for Type I letter grades) which tell us anything about an examinee's knowledge of test content *per se*. We can understand their natural appeal to the school teacher who wants to consider what students achieve according to predetermined standards of quality. On the other hand, many teachers come to realize that these predetermined levels of quality are not so objective and unchanging as might be desired, for the apparent achievement level of students can be altered tremendously by writing either easier or harder test questions over the same subject-matter unit. Many experienced teachers use a *J*-factor to "jack up" scores (by adding a few points to everyone's score) when scores have been very low. Over the years many teachers have come to believe that it is more meaningful to base test scores on a system which considers the performance of a student in comparison with others.

Do not confuse percentage-correct scores with percentile ranks.

Type I B. Letter Grades (Sometimes)

The basis for the assignment of *letter grades* at most schools and colleges is stated in terms of percentage-correct scores. Thus letter grades are one of our most common types of score. Although they may be determined on some comparative basis (Type II B 3), letter grades are more commonly Type I. Often the grading system of a school or college will state something like the following: A for 90 to 100; B for 80 to 90, etc., where the numbers refer to average percentage correct on classroom tests. Some teachers have absolute faith in such a system. I have even known a teacher to refuse an A to a student whose semester average was "only 89.9," even though two or three slightly easier (or even clearer) questions on the final examination would have put the student above 90.0.

The basic rationale, advantages, and limitations of letter grades are the same as for percentage-correct scores. The only important difference between these scores is that letter grades are expressed in coarser units. Because of this, letter grades cannot reflect small differences in ability; but, by the same token, they are not likely to differ greatly from hypothetical true scores. Note, however, that even a single unit of change is relatively large.

Type I letter grades are found by either of two methods: (1) direct grading according to judged quality (as is often done in grading essay examinations); or (2) conversion from percentage correct scores to letter grades, following a predetermined schedule as in the school and college grading system mentioned above.

When letter grades are assigned with strict adherence to quality standards (without any consideration to relative performance within the group), they are determined more by test difficulty than by anything else.

> "Don't take 'Introductory' from Jones," I heard a student say the other day. "He doesn't know that the letter A exists." I have known such teachers. Haven't you? Two teachers of the same subject to students of similar ability may differ greatly in the number of A's, F's, etc. given.

No type of score is perfect. But Type I letter grades are worse than most others because they really depend more on test difficulty than on true quality of performance (their apparent basis).

Compare with Type II B 3 letter grades.

TYPE II: INTERINDIVIDUAL COMPARISONS

Type II scores are much more commonly used with standardized tests than with classroom tests. Almost all standardized tests use some version of Type II A, B, or D scores in their norms tables. Types II A and B may be used with typical-performance tests as well as with maximum-performance tests; however, we shall be concerned here largely with their use in the latter instance.

Type II scores are relatively independent of content difficulty, for they base an examinee's score on the performance of others in a comparative (or normative) group. If the test content is inherently difficult, any specified person's score is likely to be lower than on an easier test; however, this difficulty of content will also affect the scores of the other examinees. This makes it possible to use the same test for individuals (and for groups) ranging widely in level of ability. It also permits the test constructor to aim for test items of about 50 per cent difficulty, the best difficulty level from a measurement point of view because it permits the largest number of interindividual discriminations. On the other hand, all Type II scores are influenced by the *level* of the comparison group; e.g., I will score higher when compared with college freshmen than when compared with college professors.

Type II A: Interindividual Comparison
Considering Mean and Standard Deviation

In Type II A scores, we find that interindividual comparison is expressed as the number of standard deviations between any specified score and the mean. As with all Type II scores, a change in comparison group will influence the level of score.

Type II A scores are all linear standard scores. They are called *standard* because they are based on the standard deviation; we shall see shortly why they are *linear*. They may be viewed as statements of standard-deviation distance from the mean; or they may be seen as scores which have been given a substitute mean and standard deviation. All Type II A scores have properties which make them more valuable in research than most other derived scores: (1) for every test and every group, each Type II A score gives the same mean and standard deviation; (2) they retain the shape of the raw-score distribution, changing only the calibration numbers; (3) they permit intergroup or intertest comparisons that are not possible with most other types of score; (4) they can be treated mathematically in ways that some other scores cannot be.

1. z-Score

The basic standard score is z. All other linear standard scores may be established directly from it. It tells in simple terms the difference (or distance) between a stated group's mean and any specified raw-score value.

FORMULA:

$$z = \frac{X - \overline{X}}{s}, \text{ where}$$

$X =$ a specified raw score
$\overline{X} =$ mean raw score for some group
$s =$ standard deviation of that same group.

(Thus, if z-scores are found for each examinee in the comparison group, the mean will be 0.00 and the standard deviation will be 1.00.)

EXAMPLE:

Katie Kates had a score of 49. She is to be compared with other local examinees; the mean and standard deviation of this group are 40 and 6, respectively. Katie's z-score $= (49 - 40)/6 = 9/6 = 1.5$. In other words, Katie's score is 1.5 standard deviations above the mean of this comparison group. (Assuming a normal distribution, we find that she did as well as or better than about 93 per cent of this group.)

Although z-scores have many advantages for the research worker, they are not too handy for the test user, except as a step in computing other types of linear standard score. By their very nature, about one-half of all z-scores are negative and all z-scores need to be expressed to one or two decimal positions. All other linear standard scores have been designed to eliminate the decimal point and obtain smaller units (by multiplying each z-score by a constant) and to eliminate the negative values (by adding a constant value to each z-score).

2. T-Score

The T-score is one of the most common linear standard scores. Its rationale is the same as for the z-score, except that it is made to have a mean of 50 and a standard deviation of 10.

FORMULA:

$$T = 10z + 50, \text{ where}$$
$$z = \frac{X - \overline{X}}{s}, \text{ as shown above}$$
$$10 = \text{a multiplying constant (i.e., each } z\text{-score is}$$
$$\text{multiplied by 10)}$$
$$50 = \text{an additive constant (i.e., 50 is added to each}$$
$$\text{value of } 10z).$$

EXAMPLE:

Katie Kates' z-score was 1.5; therefore, her T-score $= 10 \ (1.5) + 50 = 15 + 50 = 65$. [Assuming a normal distribution, we find that she did as well as or better than about 93 per cent of her comparison group. In any event (normal distribution or not), her T-score of 65 is directly under her z-score of 1.5 (*see* Chart 2).]

The *T*-score has much the same advantages and limitations as does the *z*-score. It is somewhat less useful than *z* for certain research purposes, but it is more convenient to interpret since there are no negative values. (The probability of obtaining a value which is more than five standard deviations below the mean in a normal distribution is less than one three-millionth.) Nor do we typically use decimals with *T*-scores.

Unfortunately *T*-scores are easily confused with certain other types of score, especially the *T*-scaled score (considered shortly as a Type II B score). These two *T*'s are identical in a normal distribution, but may differ considerably in a badly skewed distribution. *T*-scores are often confused with percentile ranks, too, for they use similar numbers. The reader may wish to check these similarities and differences in Chart 2.

3. AGCT-Score

This score gets its name from the *Army General Classification Test*. It is similar to *z* and to *T*, except that it has a mean of 100 and a standard deviation of 20.

FORMULA:

$$AGCT = 20z + 100, \text{ where}$$
z = a *z*-score, as defined above; and
20 and 100 are multiplying and additive constants, respectively.

EXAMPLE:

Katie Kates' *z*-score was 1.5; therefore, her *AGCT*-score = 20 (1.5) + 100 = 30 + 100 = 130. [Assuming a normal distribution, we find that she did as well as or better than about 93 per cent of her comparison group. In any event (normal distribution or not), her *AGCT*-score of 130 is directly under her *z*-score of 1.5 and her *T*-score of 65 (*see* Chart 2).]

As originally used, the *AGCT*-score was based on a large sample of soldiers who took the first military edition of the test; their mean was set at 100 and their standard deviation at 20. Subsequent editions of the test have been made to give comparable results. These scores are very similar to the deviation IQ's which will be considered shortly. It should be noted, however, that AGCT's have a standard deviation somewhat larger than commonly used with IQ's. Although a convenient scale, *AGCT*-scores are not in general use except in connection with the military and civilian editions of the *Army General Classification Test*.

4. CEEB-Score

This score was developed for the purpose of reporting the results of the *College Entrance Examination Board* tests and is used by the Educational Testing Service as the basis for reported scores on many of its other special-program tests. It is similar to other linear standard scores, but has a mean of 500 and a standard deviation of 100.

FORMULA:

$$CEEB = 100z + 500, \text{ where}$$
$$z = \text{a } z\text{-score, as defined above.}$$

EXAMPLE:

Katie Kates' z-score of 1.5 would be expressed on this CEEB scale as 650. (Her percentile rank would be 93, assuming a normal distribution. In any distribution, her *CEEB*-score of 650 lies directly under a z of 1.5, a T of 65, etc.).

As originally used, the *CEEB*-scores were set up differently each year according to the mean and standard deviation of that year's examinees. They now are keyed to the mean and standard deviation of 1941's examinees, so that it is possible to compare results from one year to the next. Note, however, that because *CEEB*-scores are not based on the present set of examinees, the Educational Testing Service also reports percentile ranks which are based on current examinees.

5. Deviation IQ's (Sometimes)

The *IQ* (*Intelligence Quotient*) suggested about fifty years ago by the German psychologist Stern sounded very reasonable; Terman used it with the *Stanford-Binet* in 1916, and soon other test constructors began using it. Very few tests still use the ratio IQ (a Type III score) where IQ is based on the ratio of mental age to chronological age. One big advantage of a deviation IQ is that it has a common standard deviation for all ages covered by the test on which it is determined.

The term, deviation IQ, is used to describe three different types of score. We shall deal here with the first meaning, a linear standard score (but see also Type II B 4 e and Type IV C). The deviation IQ has the same advantages and limitations as other linear standard scores except that it has a mean of 100 and a standard deviation as fixed by the test's author. We shall mention briefly the deviation IQ on the *Wechsler* intelligence tests and on the 1960 edition of the *Stanford-Binet;* earlier editions of the *Stanford-Binet* used a ratio IQ (Type III A).

(*a*) *Wechsler* IQ's.   Two of the most common individual tests of intelligence are the *Wechsler Intelligence Scale for Children* (WISC) and the *Wechsler Adult Intelligence Scale* (WAIS). Although they differ in some respects, their IQ's are determined in somewhat similar fashion, and we will illustrate with the WAIS. There are six verbal subtests and five performance subtests, which combine to yield a Verbal IQ, a Performance IQ, and a Total IQ. Seven different norms groups are used to cover the age range from sixteen to sixty-four years.

A raw score is found for each of the eleven subtests. Each subtest score is converted to a normalized standard score (see Type II B 4 e on page 118) with a mean of 10 and a standard deviation of 3. The sum of these eleven normalized standard scores is found. This sum of scores is converted to a deviation IQ with the aid of a table (a separate table for each of the seven different age groups).

In constructing the test, the mean and standard deviation of subtest-sums were found for each of the seven age groups. The author had decided in advance that he wanted his test to have a mean of 100 and a standard deviation of 15. Therefore, though separately for each age group, he used the formula: $IQ = 15z + 100$. The WAIS user now need only consult the appropriate table to find the IQ value which corresponds to the sum of the subtest scores. Verbal and Performance IQ's are found in the same manner, but are based on only their six and five subtests, respectively.

(*b*) 1960 *Stanford-Binet* IQ's.   Until the 1960 revision, *Stanford-Binet* (S-B) IQ's were ratio IQ's; in fact, it was the first test on which IQ's were ever used. The authors of the 1960 revision decided to adopt the deviation IQ so that the standard deviation would be constant from age to age; in spite of careful and extensive effort in preparing the previous revision (1937), standard deviations for different ages had differed by as much as eight IQ points!

The *Stanford-Binet* has tasks arranged by age levels from two years to superior adult. Following carefully described procedures, the examiner finds a mental age from the test. This MA is entered into a table opposite the examinee's chronological age (an adjusted age, of course, for adults) and the IQ is found.

For each chronological age group of examinees, the authors found the mean and standard deviation of MA's. The mean MA found was set equal to an IQ of 100 for people of that specified CA. The authors then found the MA that was one standard deviation below the mean; that was set equal to an IQ of 84. One standard deviation above the mean was set equal to 116, etc.

In the case of the S-B, then, we have a linear standard score with a mean of 100 and a standard deviation of 16. Separately for each chronological age group, the authors have used the formula: $IQ = 16z + 100$. The scale employed is thus very similar to that used on the *Wechsler* tests, as may be seen in Figure 10 of Chart 2. (Note, however, that IQ's found for the same examinee on the two tests might still differ; in addition to error in measurement, the tests also differ in content and in their norms groups.)

SUMMARY: LINEAR STANDARD SCORES   All linear standard scores tell us the location of an examinee's raw score in relation to the mean of some specified group and in terms of the group's standard deviation. In any distribution, normal or not, we can convert freely from raw-score values to linear standard-score equivalents without in any way changing the shape of the original distribution. Because of these properties, we can average these scores exactly as we can raw scores; we cannot average other Type II scores.

Type II B: Interindividual Comparison
Considering Rank

Like Type II A scores, these are very commonly used in reporting standardized test results. Unlike Type II A scores, they are based on the number of people with scores higher (or lower) than a specified score value. We lose all information about distance away from the mean, etc. On the other hand, some of these scores (especially Type II B 4) have the effect of creating a distribution which is more nearly normal than the distribution of raw scores on which they are based. As with all other scores (except Type I), values will change for different comparison groups.

1. Rank

The simplest possible statement of relative position is rank: first for highest or best, second for next, third for next, . . . , etc. It has the unique disadvantage of being so completely bound by the number of cases that it is never used formally in reporting test results.

2. Percentile Rank and Percentile Band

The percentile rank (sometimes called centile rank) is probably the score used most frequently in reporting the results of standardized tests. All things considered, it is probably the best type for general use in test interpretation; however, it does have limitations as we shall see presently.

A percentile is any one of the ninety-nine points which divide a frequency distribution into one hundred groups of equal size. A percentile rank is a person's relative position within a specified group.

> We find the percentile rank of an examinee or of a given raw-score value. We find a specified percentile value by finding its equivalent raw-score value. Thus a raw score of 162 may have a percentile rank of 44; the forty-fourth percentile will be a raw score of 162.

Because of the importance of percentiles and percentile ranks, Chart 3 has been included to describe and illustrate their computation. The raw-score values used were selected deliberately not to conflict with the numbers used to express any of the more common derived scores. The range in raw scores is certainly less than we would expect to find for most groups; this, too, was done deliberately in order to simplify the presentation.

CHART 3

Computation of Percentiles and Percentile Ranks

1 X	2 f	3 cf	4 cf_{mp}	5 cP_{mp}	6 PR
225	1	50	49.5	99.0	99
224	1	49	48.5	97.0	97
223	2	48	47.0	94.0	94
222	4	46	44.0	88.0	88
221	2	42	41.0	82.0	82
220	5	40	37.5	75.0	75
219	6	35	32.0	64.0	64
218	8	29	25.0	50.0	50
217	5	21	18.5	37.0	37
216	4	16	14.0	28.0	28
215	4	12	10.0	20.0	20
214	4	8	6.0	12.0	12
213	3	4	2.5	6.0	6
212	0	1	1.0	2.0	2
211	1	1	0.5	1.0	1

Symbols Used Above:

1 X = value of raw score
2 f = frequency (number of examinees making this score)
3 cf = cumulative frequency
4 cf_{mp} = cf to midpoint of score
5 cP_{mp} = cumulative percentage to midpoint of score
6 PR = percentile rank for the specified raw-score value

To Find PR's for Stated Raw-Score Values

1. List every possible *raw-score value*.
2. Find the *frequency* with which each score occurs.
3. Find the *cumulative frequency* up through each score by adding that score's frequency to the frequencies of all lower scores; e.g., cf through score of 214 (i.e., through its upper limit, 214.5): $4 + 3 + 0 + 1 = 8$.
4. Find the *cumulative frequency to midpoint* of each score by adding one-half of frequency at the score to cumulative frequency up through next lower score; e.g., cf_{mp} for 212.0: $(\frac{1}{2} \times 0) + 1 = 1.0$; cf_{mp} for 216.0: $(\frac{1}{2} \times 4) + 12 = 14.0$.
5. Convert to *cumulative percentage* by the formula: $cP_{mp} = 100(cf_{mp})/N$, where: cP_{mp} and cf_{mp} are defined as above, and N = number of cases;

or, use $100/N$ as a constant to multiply by successive cf_{mp} values, as here: $100/N = 100/50 = 2.0$.

6. Find *percentile ranks* by rounding these cP_{mp} values to nearest whole numbers (except use *1−* for *0* and *99+* for *100*.)

To Find Raw-Score Equivalents of Stated Percentile Values

1. Prepare Columns 1–3, as above.
2. Change from *percentile* to *number of cases* by multiplying it by $N/100$; e.g., in finding P_{20}: $20 \times 50/100 = 10$.
3. Count up through the *number of cases* found in Step 2, assuming that cases are distributed evenly across each score; i.e., one third of the cases at a score lie one third of the way between real lower limit and real upper limit of score, one quarter of the cases lie one quarter of the way through score, etc. See examples below.
4. Corresponding *raw-score* value is the desired *percentile*.

Examples:

Find P_{30}, the raw-score value at or below which fall 30% of the cases:

A. 30% of fifty cases = $30 \times 50/100 = 15$; we must count up through 15 cases.
B. Find the biggest number in the *cf* column that is *not greater than* 15—i.e., *12*.
C. Subtract number found in Step B from number of cases needed: $15 − 12 = 3$.
D. We need to get these cases from those cases at next higher score; in other words, we need three of the four cases at score of *216*.
E. We go that fractional way through the score: $\frac{3}{4}$, or $.75 + 215.5$ (real lower limit of score) = *216.25*. $P_{30} = 216.25$.

Find P_{50} (the median):

A. 50% of fifty cases is 25.
B. We note *25* in the cf_{mp} column; P_{50} = midpoint of the score, *218*, or *218.0*.

Find P_{80}, the eightieth percentile:

A. 80% of fifty cases is 40.
B. We note *40* in the *cf* column; P_{80} = upper limit of the score, *220*, or *220.5*.

We should note that in Chart 3 we have found cumulative frequencies up to the midpoint of each raw-score value, and have translated these cf_{mp} values into percentages which, rounded to whole numbers, are the percentile ranks.

I hope that this paragraph is not confusing. I wish that it could be omitted. Some test publishers base percentile norms, not on cumulative frequencies to the midpoint as we have, but on cumulative frequencies to the upper limits of each score. Still others who work with tests base their percentile norms on cumulative frequencies up to the lower limits of each score. I dislike these latter two methods for three reasons: (1) they are confusing and ambiguous; (2) they produce percentile ranks that are incompatible with percentile values; and, (3) they more logically are percentile ranks for limits of scores, rather than for midpoints of scores (e.g., a percentile rank for a score of 213.5 or 214.5, rather than 214.0). We find that some test manuals state which procedure has been followed. More often, though, manuals say nothing about which procedure was followed, and the reader is left wondering. Please note, however, that only when the range is small (say, less than twenty-thirty score-units) do the differences in procedure make much practical difference.

Advantages and Limitations of Percentile Ranks.   The principal advantage of PR's lies in their ease of interpretation. Even a person who thinks of percentiles as being equally spaced (which they could not be unless the same number of persons obtained each raw score) can understand something about these scores if he knows only that a PR is a statement of the percentage of cases in a specified group who fall at or below a given score value.

On the other hand, we find it very easy to overemphasize differences near the median and to underemphasize differences near the extremes; in Figure 10 of Chart 2, we should note the slight difference between PR's of 40 and 50 as compared with PR's of 90 and 99. And even these varying differences are altered when a distribution departs markedly from the normal probability model, as may be seen in Figure 11 of the chart.

Averaging Percentile Ranks.   Because interpercentile distances are not equal, we cannot average them directly (as we could Type II A scores). This point applies equally against averaging the performance of one person on two or more tests and against averaging the performance of a group of people on one test.

To find the average PR of one person on several tests: convert each PR 'to a z-score, using Table 9 in the Appendix; average the z-scores; convert the average z to a PR. Note: this method assumes a normal distribution for each test and the same normative group for each test; only slight errors will be introduced if the distributions are nearly normal, but the averaging cannot be done if the PR's are based on different groups.

To find the average PR for a group of persons on one test: average the raw scores; find the PR corresponding to this average raw score. Note: this method is one we might follow to find how our local group compares with a national normative group; there would be no point in doing this with the same group on which the norms were based. Note further that this procedure gives the PR corresponding to the average raw score. Since group averages vary less than do individual raw scores, the value found should never be thought of as the PR of the group (in comparison to other groups).

More Advantages and Limitations.   With percentiles, we are using a common scale of values for all distributions on all tests. Regardless of the range of raw scores, the range of PR's will be the same: 0 or 1— to 100 or 99+ (unless more than 0.5 per cent of the examinees make either the lowest possible score or the highest possible score). On very short tests, a difference of twenty or thirty PR's may represent a difference of only one or two raw-score values as we may note in Chart 3.

Some publishers use PR's of 0 and 100; some do not. This reflects a philosophical issue:

> Lazilu Lucas has a score lower than anyone in the normative group. A PR of 0 would certainly describe her performance. On the other hand, we like to think of a normative group as being a sample representative of a large population. If Lazilu is being compared with an appropriate group, she presumably belongs to the population from which the normative group was taken. It is not logical to say that she did less well than everyone in the population of which she is part. Following this line of reasoning, I prefer to use 1— instead of 0 and 99+ instead of 100.

By now some readers will wonder how this issue can exist if a percentile rank is one of the ninety-nine points which divide a frequency distribution into one hundred groups of equal size as defined a few pages ago.

Figure 12 gives us the answer. If we divide the ranked distribution of scores into one hundred subgroups of equal size, as shown across the top of the line, there are ninety-nine percentile points setting off the one hundred subgroups. In expressing a percentile rank, however, we round to the nearest whole percentile value—as

Figure 12. Graphic Explanation of Percentile Ranks at Upper and Lower Extremes of a Distribution. (See further explanation in the text.)

shown by lines drawn across the bottom of the line to indicate the real limits of each percentile rank. Ninety-nine of these units leave 0.5 per cent left over at each extreme of the distribution: it is these extremes that we call 1— and 99+.

One final disadvantage of percentile ranks is that they use a scale of numbers that is shared with several other types of score: percentage-correct scores, *T*-scores, and IQ's. There is the possibility of confusion, especially with percentage-correct scores; we must remember that percentage-correct scores are based on percentage of content, whereas PR's are based on percentage of cases in a specified group.

SUMMARY OF PERCENTILE RANKS   Although PR's have many limitations, they are very commonly used in expressing the results of standardized tests. They are reasonably easy to understand and to explain to others. Considering all advantages and limitations, PR's are probably the best single derived score for general use in expressing test results. Consider, too, the following application.

A New Application of Percentile Ranks: The Percentile Band

An interesting new application of percentile ranks is to be found in the percentile band now being used by the Educational Testing Service with some of its newer tests. As the name suggests, the percentile band is a band or range of percentile ranks. The upper limit of the band corresponds to the percentile rank for a score one standard error of measurement above the obtained score, and the lower limit of the band corresponds to the percentile rank for a score one standard error of measurement below the obtained score.

The purpose of this application of course is to emphasize to every user of the test that measurement error is present in each score. The percentile band is useful, too, in interpreting differences between different tests within the same test battery.

I believe that this approach has considerable merit and hope that it may come into widespread use. It seems to combine the stated advantages of the percentile rank with an emphasis that the score should not be treated as a precise value. In addition, it seems to have the advantages of other coarse-unit scores while avoiding their principal limitation (i.e., that a single unit of change is relatively large) by centering the band on the obtained score—thereby changing the limits of the band only slightly for slight differences in score.

This may prove to be the most valuable single type of score for general test interpretation purposes.

3. Letter Grades (Sometimes)

As suggested earlier, *letter grades* may be based on comparative performance; when so used, they are a Type II B score. A few standardized tests use such scores, each clearly indicating those values to be assigned A's, those to be assigned B's, etc. Far more commonly, a teacher will use some interindividual comparison in assigning course grades.

Note that it is not necessary to decide in advance how many students will receive each letter grade. "Grading on the curve" is rather old-fashioned anyway. The practice of basing letter grades on a normal curve (perhaps by giving 10 per cent A, 20 per cent B, 40 per cent C, 20 per cent D, and 10 per cent F) is indefensible unless one has very large numbers of unselected students. One way of assigning grades on the basis of comparative performance that I like is as follows:

> I make no assumption about the number of students who will fail or who will get any particular grade. I do assume that I will give at least a single A (and actually give more, usually). During the semester, I give several quizzes and make certain that the standard deviation of each is about the same (for tests "weight" themselves according to size of standard deviation). I make the standard deviation of the final examination about twice those of the quizzes. I add these raw scores and arrange the students in order of summed scores. I may even draw a histogram similar to Figure 1 so that I may see how each student compares with every other student.

Oftentimes the results will show several clusters of students—suggesting that they be given the same grade. If there are several students whose summed scores seem almost "to drop out" of the distribution, these may receive F's. I will, however, consider carefully whether any of these students has shown a little promise—perhaps by great improvement on the final examination—that might justify some grade other than F. I try to be a little more generous with higher grades when my class has been a bit better than average (as the year when three of my thirty students made Phi Beta Kappa); some years my students seem less promising, and I am more cautious about assigning many high grades.

I think that every teacher recognizes that grades are somewhat arbitrary and subjective. I try to make the grades I assign as fair as possible, reflecting comparative performance for the most part—but with just a dash of consideration for the sort of class I have.

This grading scheme works fairly well for me. I am not proposing that it is ideal—but let me know if you ever do find the *perfect* grading system, won't you?

4. Normalized Standard Scores (Area Transformations)

Normalized standard scores are derived scores which are assigned standard-score-like values, but which are computed more like percentile ranks. With linear standard scores, the shape of the distribution of raw scores is reproduced faithfully; if additional baselines were drawn for a frequency polygon, we would find that values of any of those standard scores would lie in a straight line below the corresponding raw-score values regardless of the shape of the raw-score distribution. With normalized standard scores this is true only when the raw-score distribution is normal—as shown in Figure 11.

As suggested by their name, normalized standard scores have the property of making a distribution a closer approximation of the normal probability distribution. This is accomplished in similar fashion for all normalized standard scores, so we shall consider the general procedure here rather than treating it separately for each score.

Computing normalized standard scores. The following procedure is used in computing normalized standard scores:

1. List every possible raw-score value.
2. Find the frequency with which each score occurs.
3. Find the cumulative frequency up through each score.

4. Find the cumulative frequency up to the midpoint of each score.
5. Convert the cumulative frequencies to cumulative percentages.

(NOTE: Steps 1-5 are identical with the first five steps in finding PR's; this procedure is shown in Chart 3.)

6. Substitute the normalized standard score value that is appropriate for this cumulative percentage in a normal probability distribution. These values, different for each normalized standard score, may be found from Table 9 in the Appendix.

Area transformations. As we can see from the computation procedures above, these scores are known as *area transformations* because they are based on standard-score values that would correspond to specified cumulative percentages in a normal distribution (and area, we recall from Chapter Four, indicates frequency or percentage of cases).

> To say that 23 per cent of the cases lie below a specified score is the same as saying that the 23 per cent of the area of a graph showing that distribution lies below that same score value. In finding a normalized standard score, we are merely substituting for that score value a standard-score-like value that would be at a point where 23 per cent of the normal curve's area falls below it.

(*a*) T-*Scaled Score.* In a normal distribution, this has exactly the same properties as the *T*-score (including its mean of 50 and standard deviation of 10). In fact, this present score is called *T*-score more commonly than *T*-scaled score. It has all the advantages and limitations of the normalized standard scores mentioned above. It has the additional limitation of being confused with the *T*-score, a fact which is of practical significance only when the distribution of raw scores deviates appreciably from the normal probability model.

(*b*) *Stanine Scores.* Developed by World War II psychologists for use with the U. S. Air Force, *stanine scores* were intended to maximize the information about test performance that could be entered into a single column of an IBM punched card. Obviously one card could hold more one-digit scores than two- or three-digit scores. Whereas earlier standard scores had indicated specific values, stanines (from *sta*ndard score of *nine* units) were intended to represent bands of values; except for the open-ended extreme stanines of 1 and 9, each stanine was to equal one-half standard deviation in width and the mean was to be the midpoint of the middle stanine, 5.

Apparently some Air Force psychologists used the stanine as a linear standard score at first, thereby giving it exactly the properties mentioned above; however, others treated it as a normalized standard score, and it is so used today. When distributed normally, stanines will have a mean of 5 and a standard deviation of about 2; in addition, all stanines except 1 and 9 will be exactly one-half standard deviation in width. With distributions which are not normal, of course, these values will only be approximated.

As a normalized standard score, its values for any distribution are determined by: (1) following steps 1-5 of the general procedure shown on pages 114-115; (2) assigning a stanine value to each raw score according to this table:

Lowest 4%	Next 7%	Next 12%	Next 17%	Middle 20%	Next 17%	Next 12%	Next 7%	Highest 4%
Stanine 1	Stanine 2	Stanine 3	Stanine 4	Stanine 5	Stanine 6	Stanine 7	Stanine 8	Stanine 9

At least one publisher (Harcourt, Brace & World, Inc.) is promoting the general use of stanines in test interpretation. In addition to using these scores in some of its own norms tables, the publisher points out the relative ease of using them in preparing local norms for both standardized and classroom tests. When finding stanines for our own distributions, we may have to approximate the above figures; we must assign the same stanine value to everyone obtaining the same raw score, and it is unlikely that our cumulative percentages will allow us to follow the table precisely.

In general, stanines have the advantages and limitations of other coarse-unit scores. It is unlikely that a person's obtained score is many units away from his true score, but a test interpreter is perhaps more likely to put undue confidence in the accuracy of the obtained score.

Table 9 in the Appendix shows stanine values and equivalent values in a normal distribution. (*See also* Chart 2.)

Flanagan's Extended Stanine Scores. For use in reporting scores on his *Flanagan Aptitude Classification Tests,* Flanagan splits each stanine value into three units by using plus and minus signs; stanine 1 is made into three stanine values: 1—, 1, and 1+, and every other stanine is treated similarly. In this way Flanagan achieves a twenty-seven-unit normalized standard score scale. His scale has certain obvious advantages over the usual stanine scale, but it is not in general use. The percentile equivalents of these extended stanine values differ slightly for each test in the FACT battery; they may be found in the FACT *Examiner's Manual.*

(*c*) *C-Scaled Score.* Guilford has proposed the use of a *C*-scale which provides one additional unit at each end of the stanine scale. The *C*-scale has eleven units assigned values of 0 through 10. This scale is used in the norms tables of tests published by the Sheridan Supply Company. *C*-scores are computed exactly as are stanines, except that the values given are as shown in this table:

Lowest 1%	Next 3%	Next 7%	Next 12%	Next 17%	Middle 20%	Next 17%	Next 12%	Next 7%	Next 3%	Highest 1%
$C = 0$	$C = 1$	$C = 2$	$C = 3$	$C = 4$	$C = 5$	$C = 6$	$C = 7$	$C = 8$	$C = 9$	$C = 10$

(*d*) *Sten Scores.* Similar in rationale to the two preceding scores is the *sten* (a normalized *s*tandard score with *ten* units). This system provides for five normalized standard-score units on each side of the mean, each being one-half standard deviation in width except for stens of 1 and 10 which are open-ended. Since it is a normalized standard score, these interval sizes apply exactly only in a normal distribution. This scale is used for norms of some of Cattell's *Institute for Personality and Ability Testing* tests, published by the Bobbs-Merrill Company. Stens may be computed in the same way as stanines, except that the values given are as shown in this table:

Lowest 2%	Next 5%	Next 9%	Next 15%	Low Middle 19%	High Middle 19%	Next 15%	Next 9%	Next 5%	Highest 2%
Sten 1	Sten 2	Sten 3	Sten 4	Sten 5	Sten 6	Sten 7	Sten 8	Sten 9	Sten 10

(*e*) *Deviation IQ's (Sometimes).*   Although no well-known intelligence test (to the best of my knowledge) presently uses deviation IQ in this normalized standard-score sense, such a use will probably come before long. Such deviation IQ's would have the same general advantages and limitations as the *T*-scaled scores, except that their mean would be 100 and their standard deviation would be as determined by the author and publisher. In all other characteristics, they would resemble the deviation IQ (Type II A 5).

Wechsler subtests. Something similar to deviation IQ's of the sort mentioned in the previous paragraph is already found in the subtests (or scales) of the *Wechsler Adult Intelligence Scale* and the *Wechsler Intelligence Scale for Children.* Each of the separate scales on both of these tests uses a normalized standard score with a mean of 10 and a standard deviation of 3; however, these scale scores are used principally to find total scores on which the Wechsler IQ's (Type II A 5 a) are based, and are rarely interpreted in themselves.

(*f*) *ITED-scores.*   One final type of normalized standard score will be mentioned. The *ITED*-score was developed for use with the *Iowa Tests of Educational Development,* but is now also used with the *National Merit Scholarship Qualifying Examination* and other tests. This score is given a mean of 15 and a standard deviation of 5 and is based on a nationally representative sample of tenth- and eleventh-grade students.

5. Decile Ranks

Cattell also uses what he calls decile scores in some of his norms tables. In common usage, a *decile* is defined as being any one of nine points separating the frequency distribution into ten groups of equal size. Thus, the first decile (D_1) equals the tenth percentile, D_2 equals the twentieth percentile, etc. Cattell modifies this meaning of decile to include a band (or range) of 10 per cent of the cases—5 per cent on each side of the actual decile point; for example, Cattell's decile score of 1 includes values from the fifth to fifteenth percentiles. (Values below P_5 are given a decile score of 0; values above P_{95}, a score of 10.) Cattell believes that these scores should be used in preference to percentile ranks when the range in raw scores is very small. In order to prevent confusion between decile and decile score (and to point out their similarity to percentile ranks), I prefer to use the term decile ranks.

Type II C: Interindividual Comparison
Considering Range

Only one derived score, the per cent placement score, is based on interindividual comparisons considering the range of raw scores. So far as I know, it is used in rare instances to express scores on classroom tests of achievement—and nowhere else.

1. Per Cent Placement Score

The *per cent placement* score indicates a person's position on a 101-point scale where the highest score made is set at 100 and the lowest at 0.

FORMULA:

$$X_{\%pl} = 100 \frac{(X - L)}{(H - L)} \text{, where}$$

X = any specified raw score
L = the lowest raw score made
H = the highest raw score made.

EXAMPLE:

On a 300-item test, there is a range from 260 to 60; range $= H - L$ $= 260 - 60 = 200$. Barry's raw score was 60; his per cent placement score is 0. Harry's raw score was 260; his $X_{\%pl} = 100$. Larry's raw score was 140; his $X_{\%pl} = 40$ [i.e., 100 (140 − 60)/200 = 40].

Type II D: Interindividual Comparison Considering
Status of Those Making Same Score

Type II D scores include age scores and grade-placement scores. These are set up to express test performance in terms of averages of groups which differ in status (either in chronological age or in grade placement). Thus the examinee's score is not a statement of how well he has done when compared with some single specified group, but rather a statement of which group (among several that differ in level) he is presumably most like.

Type II D scores are used most commonly with standardized tests of achievement and intelligence for children of school age. They are not suited for use with informal, local tests.

Although Type II D scores seem easy to understand, they have many limitations which are not immediately apparent.

1. Age Scores

Age scores may be developed for any human characteristic that changes with age; however, they are used most frequently with intelligence and achievement tests for children of school age or below. The most common age score is the *mental age* (MA), a concept developed by Alfred Binet about sixty years ago for use with the earliest successful intelligence test.

An age score is an expression of an examinee's test performance stated in terms of the developmental level characteristic of the average child of that corresponding chronological age.

> Karl gets an MA of seven years six months (expressed as: 7–6) on an intelligence test. This means that Karl's level of performance is equal to the mean score made by children with a chronological age of 7–6. Alternatively, though less frequently, an MA may be defined as the average chronological age of individuals making a given raw score. By this definition, Karl's MA of 7–6 would indicate that the average chronological age of children with the same raw score as his was 7–6.

When used with young children, age scores are reasonably easy to understand. The logic is straightforward and simple. On the other hand, age scores are easily overinterpreted. A five-year-old who obtains an age score of 7 on a test is still only five years of age in most respects. There can be no assumption that all people with the same age score have identical abilities.

Test makers have difficulty in getting good representative samples for age norms, because some children are located a grade or two ahead of (or behind) their age peers. These youngsters must be included if the norms are to be meaningful, but they are especially difficult to locate when they attend other schools. For example, some bright youngsters may enter junior high school one or two years ahead of their age peers, while dull ones may be transferred to special classes at other schools.

An age score by itself tells us little about the individual's achievement or potentiality, even though it may be used in combination with chronological age or other measure to form a quotient score that will do so.

(*a*) *Mental Age.*   Although the MA served Binet's need for a score that could be understood easily, it has been extended beyond reason.

As originally conceived, MA units were credited to a child for each task he passed. The sum of these units gave him an MA; this MA had the property of being equal *on the average* to chronological age.

On certain intelligence tests, though, MA's are determined by finding first the number of items correct; then, an MA is assigned according to the chronological age group for which that score is the average. When used in this manner, MA is merely an extra step in computing an Intelligence Quotient (IQ).

Still another unwarranted extension of the MA has been its application to adults. Although there is increasing evidence that at least some aspects of intelligence may continue to grow on into middle age, it is also true that the increment between successive ages becomes smaller with increasing age. There are more obvious mental differences between ages of 6 and 7 than between 16 and 17 or between 26 and 27. Even within the age range of 5 to 15, there is no basis for believing that MA units are equal in size. An age-scale approach is not feasible beyond the middle teen years; and, on tests where an age-scale is used, all people beyond a given chronological age level are treated (in computing an IQ) as having the same chronological age. Any MA's reported as being above sixteen or seventeen years are necessarily for the convenience of the test— rather than a reflection of the typical performance of people with those higher chronological ages. Some people, for example, will obtain scores which are higher than the mean for *any* age group. The nature of the mean guarantees this.

In interpreting MA's, we must use considerable caution. Within the range of about five to fifteen years, MA's may be reasonably meaningful for children of approximately those same chronological ages; however, it is not correct to think of a mentally defective adult having, let us say, an MA of 6-0 as being equal to the average child of that age. The adult will have habits and motor skills which differ greatly from the typical child, whereas the child will probably be able to grasp many new ideas much more readily than the retarded adult.

One difficulty with the interpretation of MA's is the fact that the standard deviations differ from test to test and even from age to age within the same test. Therefore there is no way of generalizing age score values that are any stated distance from the mean; e.g., an MA of 13-3 for a child of 12-3 does not indicate the same degree of superiority as does an MA of 6-3 for a child of 5-3.

Mental age scores are tricky to interpret. It is easy to believe that their apparent meaning is real. In the elementary school, MA's may be useful to the teacher in her thinking about the potentialties of her pupils. Even here, she will want to refer to the school psychologist pupils who are having extreme learning difficulties. The school psychologist will probably use individual, rather than group, tests in helping to understand the children and in checking the validity of inferences made from scores on group tests. Aside from school and clinical settings, the mental age is a type of score which should not be used. In my opinion, the mental age should *never* be used in personnel and industrial settings.

(*b*) *Educational Ages, etc.*   Very similar to the mental age is the educational age. An *educational age* (EA) indicates test performance at a given level—which level is expressed as the age of individuals for whom this is average performance.

> Opal Oppleby has an EA of 8–6 on a test. In other words, her achievement on this test is equal to the average (mean or median) performance of children in the norm group who were eight years six months of age, when tested; or, less frequently, this may mean that the average chronological age of children earning the same score she did, is 8–6.

Actually, what we are calling simply educational age goes under many different names: achievement age, subject age, or [*any* subject matter] age.

All the difficulties and limitations mentioned for the MA hold for the EA at least equally as well.

> The hypothetical *Arithmetic Acuity Test* was standardized on groups of 500 children tested at each of the following chronological

ages: 7–0, 7–3, 7–6, 7–9, 8–0, 8–3, 8–6, 8–9, and 9–0. Mean raw scores were found for each of these nine age groups. Test statisticians then interpolated to find probable mean scores for each of the omitted in-between ages. (For example: the mean raw score for 7–3 was 26, and the mean for 7–0 was 20; the test manual shows 24 as equal to an arithmetic age of 7–2 and 22 as equal to an arithmetic age of 7–1.)

Obviously some children who are tested with the *Arithmetic Acuity Test* are going to earn scores which are lower than the mean for the lowest age group tested, and others are going to obtain scores higher than the mean for the oldest age group tested. To provide arithmetic ages which may be reported for such extreme cases, the test statisticians went to work again—this time extending (extrapolating) arithmetic age values at each extreme, basing estimates on educated guesses as to probable performance of older and younger groups of children. These extrapolated values are shown by the dotted line in Figure 13.

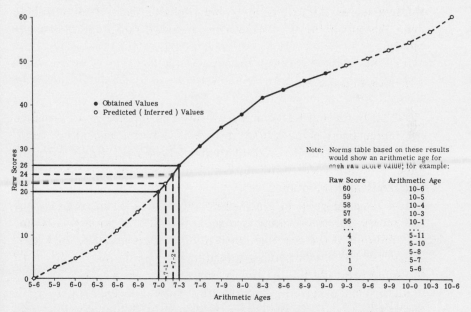

Figure 13. Illustration of Interpolated and Extrapolated Age Scores on the Hypothetical Arithmetic Acuity Test.

To some extent these extreme scores may be verified by the publisher through research with other levels of the test in articulation studies (*see* Chapter Five). At some point, however, the EA system must break down, for superior older children will earn scores which are above the average for *any* chronological age. EA values assigned at the upper limits must be arbitrary.

An assumption basic to the EA seems to be that children acquire knowledge and skill more or less uniformly throughout the calendar year—that is, that the child learns just as much per month during the long summer vacation as during the school year. Another basic assumption of EA's seems to be that age is more important in determining a child's level of test performance than is his grade placement, thereby ignoring the fact that certain skills and facts are taught at designated grades. Both assumptions are probably false.

Perhaps EA's may be of some use in comparing intra-individual variability—in deciding whether Paul has a higher arithmetic age or a higher reading age. Even in such instances, we must have evidence that the same or similar normative groups were used in developing the age scores. And there are other types of scores which will do even this job better (for example, percentile ranks and percentile bands).

2. Grade-Placement Scores

Probably the most common score used in reporting performance of standardized achievement tests is the *grade-placement* score. This is unfortunate! In spite of their intrinsic appeal and apparent logic, they are very confusing and lend themselves to all sorts of erroneous interpretations.

The basic rationale of grade-placement scores is similar to that of age scores, for their values are set to equal the average score of school pupils at the corresponding grade placement. They are established by: (1) testing youngsters at several grade placements with the same test; (2) finding the average (mean or median) for each grade-placement group; (3) plotting these averages on a graph and connecting these plots with as straight a line as possible; (4) extending (extrapolating) this line at both extremes to account for scores below and above the averages found; (5) reading off the closest grade-equivalent values for each raw-score value; (6) publishing these equivalents in tabular form.

Grade-placement scores are usually stated in tenths of a school year; e.g., 8.2 refers to second month of grade eight. (This system gives a value of 1.0 to the beginning of the first grade—which presumably is the true zero point in school grade placement.)

A basic assumption seems to be that children learn more or less uniformly throughout the school year (but that no learning occurs during the summer vacation). Although this is more reasonable than the corresponding assumption for EA's, it is far from true for all subject matters taught in school; for example, it is probably less true of reading than of arithmetic. Especially in the high school, subjects may be taught at different grade placements. Furthermore, children in school systems which are atypical in the content taught at certain grades may be penalized—or given a special advantage—when compared with youngsters from more conformative school systems.

Grade-placement scores are intrinsically appealing. It seems reasonable at first glance to think of children who stand high in comparison with others in their school grade as doing the same quality of work as youngsters slightly more advanced in school. And in a sense they are. But that does not mean that these children should be promoted immediately to a higher grade. (Why not—if they are working at that higher grade level?) Ponder, if you will: these grade-placement scores are based on the average performance of pupils having that actual placement in school. In obtaining that average, we had to have some better and some poorer scores.

Furthermore, regardless of how high a child's grade-placement score is, he has had only a given amount of time in school. And there are probably breadths and depths of understanding and competency which are closely related to the experiences and to the length of his exposure to school. A child's higher score is more likely to mean a more complete mastery of (and therefore fewer errors on) material taught at his grade. When this fact is considered, we see that the direct meaning of grade-placement scores is more apparent than real.

Grade-placement scores resulting from tests produced by different publishers are likely to give conflicting results. Not only is there the always-present likelihood of their selecting different normative samples, but the tests of different publishers are likely to place slightly different emphases on the same subject matter at the same level. For example, among grammar tests, one test may include many more questions on the use of the comma than another test does. Such differences inevitably will alter the grade-placement scores of individual pupils and of entire classes of pupils.

Because of their nature of computation, standard deviations are bound to differ for various subject matters—even when the tests are included in the same standardized achievement test battery and based on the same normative groups. Students are much more likely, for example, to have grade-placement scores which are several grade equivalents higher than their actual grade placement in reading and English than in arithmetic and science. The latter subjects depend much more on specific, school-taught skills. The result is that standard deviations are almost certain to be larger for English and reading than for arithmetic and science; similar, perhaps less extreme, differences exist for other subjects.

Test manuals of all of the major publishers of achievement tests carefully point out these differences in standard deviations. Many test users, though, do not understand the critical importance of these differences in any interpretation of scores. Among many other points, these different standard deviations reflect the greater possible range in grade-placement scores on some tests of an achievement battery than on others. Grade-placement scores on one test may extend up 4.5 grade-equivalents, as compared with only 2.5 grade-equivalents for another test in the same coordinated achievement battery.

Grade-placement scores are so confusing that a lower score on one test indicates relatively higher performance than does a higher score on another test. Because of the difference in size of standard deviations, this might easily happen: a grade-placement score of 8.5 on reading may be equal to a percentile rank of 60, but a grade-placement score of 8.2 on arithmetic fundamentals may be equal to a percentile rank of 98. Especially for higher elementary grades and beyond, grade-placement scores cannot meaningfully be compared from test to test—even within the same battery!

The difficulties noted above are accentuated when we consider subtests based on very few items. Here the chance passing or chance failing of a single test item may make the difference of one full grade equivalent. Who can get any meaning out of such a state of affairs?

All of these limitations exist even when the test difficulty level is appropriate for the pupil. If the test is so easy that a pupil answers all questions correctly on any part, we cannot know the score he should have—he might have done much better if there had been more items of appropriate difficulty for him. Thus again the paradox: tests which are too easy for a pupil give him a score which is too low. The same reasoning holds at the other extreme, too, of course.

Test publishers know the limitations of grade-placement scores and point them out carefully in their manuals. But not all test users have Ph.D.'s in educational measurement. And the more carefully the publisher documents the limitations of his tests and their scores, the less likely is the typical user to read the manual as carefully as he should. To the best of my knowledge, every major publisher includes at least some information about the equivalence of grade-placement scores to other types of score (percentiles, stanines, *T*-scores, etc.).

Test publishers have also been careful to point out that: (1) grade-placement scores based on all pupils assigned to a given grade differ from those based on only those pupils whose actual grade placement is appropriate for their age (see Modal-Age Grade-Placement Scores); (2) grade-placement scores are not standards that should be obtained by all pupils in order to be promoted; (3) separate tables are needed when comparing average grade-placement scores for different classes or schools (because averages differ less than do individual scores).

Yet these mistaken beliefs persist.

(*a*) *Full-Population Grade-Placement Scores.*   Many sets of grade-placement norms are based on all of the pupils in those classrooms used in developing the norms. This practice has been found to produce rather large standard deviations of grade-placement scores and to make the raw score corresponding to a given grade-placement score seem rather low. When all pupils are included in the normative samples, there is a fair percentage of children included who are overage for their actual grade placement (because of nonpromotion or illness) and a few who are underage for their actual grade placement.

Most publishers have taken steps to make their grade-placement norms produce results which seem to typify school classes better. They offer modal-age grade-placement norms either instead of, or in addition to, full-population norms.

(*b*) *Modal-Age Grade-Placement Scores.*   As mentioned above, there are some overage and some underage pupils in most classrooms. The presence of these pupils in classes used for normative purposes is thought to be undesirable. Most publishers now use modal-age grade-placement scores either exclusively or in addition to the full-population norms.

Modal-age indicates that only those pupils who are of about average age for their grade placement are used. The practices of publishers differ somewhat, but their aims are similar. One publisher may include all pupils who are not more than one year underage or overage for their grade placement; a second publisher may use only those pupils within three months of the modal chronological age for a specified grade placement.

Modal-age norms are, of course, a little more select. When both full-population and modal-age grade-placement norms are compared, we find that higher raw scores are needed to attain a given grade-placement score on modal-age norms. When we use standardized achievement tests and grade-placement scores, we should be certain to notice whether modal-age norms are being used.

(*c*) *Modal-Age and Modal-Intelligence Grade-Placement Scores.* A still further refinement of grade-placement scores is the practice of basing the norms only on pupils who are of near-average intelligence as well as being near-average in chronological age for actual grade placement. This should not have any pronounced effect on grade-placement values, but it is believed by the California Test Bureau to provide a better guarantee of a grade-placement score that is truly representative of average performance. The reasoning seems to be that the use of only those individuals who are near-average on an intelligence measure does away with the necessity for any assumption that low-ability and high-ability individuals will balance out to give a value that is a good average.

In developing these age- and intelligence-controlled score values, the California Test Bureau used only pupils with IQ's of 98-102, who were within three months of average age for their actual grade placement (for grades one through eight); progressively higher IQ's were used for successively higher grades.

(*d*) *Anticipated-Achievement Grade-Placement Scores.* Another concept used by the California Test Bureau in connection with its *California Achievement Tests* battery is the *anticipated-achievement grade-placement* score. This is a statement, separate for each test in the battery, of the average grade-placement score made by pupils in the norming groups who have a given grade placement and mental age. In this fashion the publishers have developed norms which are somewhat more individualized.

Unlike the other scores explained in this chapter, these are expected score values. They demand a special explanation for they are not predicted score values based on correlation techniques. Rather they are a statement of expectation based on actual empirical data.

In practice, the AAGP's are used in this fashion: (1) the *California Test of Mental Maturity* is administered to pupils and scored; (2) the *California Achievement Tests* are administered and scored; (3) a special table is entered with information as to: actual grade placement at the time of the two testings and MA obtained on the CTMM; and (4) the table is read for *Intellectual Status Index* (see score Type III B) and for AAGP's for the six achievement tests.

The *AAGP*-scores are to be thought of as expected values considering MA and actual grade placement. Each pupil's six obtained grade-placement scores are then compared with the corresponding six AAGP's in deciding whether he is achieving about as should be expected or very much above or below the expected level.

There seems to be considerable logic and careful work behind the development of the AAGP's and the modal-age and -intelligence grade-placement norms. The publisher has made grade-placement scores about as meaningful as they can be made. On the other hand, the publisher has also introduced an extremely complicated procedure with many opportunities for mistakes and misunderstandings. Although the work may be commendable, it seems formidable, too.

(*e*) *Mental Age Grade-Placement Scores.* This score is used occasionally in reporting the intelligence test performance of a school pupil. The mental age found for a pupil is translated into a grade-placement score—the grade placement for which this MA is the average.

The only advantage possible to claim for this score is that it is stated in grade-placement units—and that grade placement may be a more familiar concept than mental age. Like other Type II D scores, it has the disadvantage of telling us nothing directly about the brightness of the examinee. It has the additional limitations of other grade-placement scores. There is a degree of logic to stating achievement test scores in grade-placement units, but I can find none for expressing intelligence test scores in such units.

TYPE III: BASED ON INTRA-INDIVIDUAL COMPARISON

All Type III scores are unique in that they are based on two measurements of the same person; all are found as ratios or fractions. The first two are in current use, but the last two are in general disrepute.

Type III A: Ratio IQ (Intelligence Quotient)

Although we have considered the IQ twice before and will return to it once again (under Type IV), this is the original IQ—the one first proposed by Stern and first used by Terman nearly fifty years ago. The *ratio-type intelligence quotient* is found by the formula: $IQ = 100 \ MA/CA$, where MA is a mental age found from an intelligence test, and CA is the examinee's chronological age at the time of testing (with an adjusted CA used for older adolescents and adults). It is becoming a relatively less common score.

The rationale of the ratio-type IQ is widely understood, but its many limitations are less well known. The score depends on an assumption of equal-sized mental-age units, which may not exist. Ratio-type IQ's work reasonably well between the ages of about five to fifteen years, but tend to be of questionable value outside those approximate limits. Adult IQ's of necessity are based on artificial mental ages—as explained earlier—as well as "adjusted" chronological ages.

The most telling argument against the ratio IQ, however, is the observable fact that standard deviations are likely to differ from one age level to the next. If standard deviations are permitted to vary (and this cannot be controlled with a ratio IQ), the same IQ indicates different degrees of superiority or inferiority at different ages. The deviation IQ (Type II A or II B) is much better than the ratio IQ—so much better, in fact, that the ratio IQ is rapidly becoming extinct.

Type III B: Intellectual Status Index

A concept recently introduced by the California Test Bureau for use with its *California Test of Mental Maturity* is the *Intellectual Status Index*. This is a sort of IQ substitute with the denominator changed from a child's actual chronological age to the average chronological age of those children with his same grade placement in school.

This score is based on the premise that a pupil's score on an intelligence test is determined more by his placement in school than by his chronological age. The logic sounds reasonable, but the user should check carefully the size of standard deviation at different age levels. We must be careful, too, not to confuse ISI with IQ, especially for children who are either overage or underage in their respective grades. Further details may be found in manuals and other publications of the publisher.

Type III C: Educational Quotients

An *Educational Quotient* is found by dividing an educational age (EA) by chronological age (CA) and multiplying by 100. Just as we may have subject matter ages of all sorts, so may we have all sorts of subject matter quotients. EQ's have never been very widely used, for grade-placement scores have been preferred.

EQ's have much the same advantages and limitations as ratio IQ's, except that we can always use the pupil's actual CA. Since EQ's are used only with school-level achievement tests, we do not have the problem of working with arbitrary divisors—although of course we still have extrapolated EA's with which to contend.

Because of the limitations of EA's, we cannot make direct comparisons from one subject matter to another even when the tests have been standardized on the same groups. With even less confidence can we make any meaningful comparisons when different norming groups have been used for two or more tests.

Type III D: Accomplishment Quotients

There is almost unanimous agreement that the *Accomplishment Quotient* (AQ) (or Achievement Quotient) is a poor type of score. Not only is it based on two test scores, each with its own errors of measurement, but it gives illogical results.

It compares a pupil's achievement test score with a measure of his intelligence, and is presumed to indicate how completely he is living up to his capacity.

FORMULA:

$$AQ = 100\frac{EA}{MA}, \text{ where}$$

EA = educational age, determined by an achievement test
MA = mental age, determined by an intelligence test.

The ideal AQ is 100, indicating that a pupil is realizing his complete potential. How, then, do we explain AQ's above 100? Although logically impossible, AQ's above 100 are not unusual—suggesting that some pupils are achieving better than they are capable of achieving. A much more reasonable explanation of course is that the two scores entering into the AQ are fallible measures and that errors of measurement have combined to produce this "impossible" result.

All other Type III scores are based on one essentially error-free measure (actually measurement error is so slight that it is negligible), either CA or grade placement. These other scores then are of the same order of accuracy as are the age scores which form their numerators. With the AQ, though, both numerator and denominator values are determined by separate tests—and the AQ is subject to the measurement errors of both. The result is a remarkably poor type of score.

TYPE IV: ASSORTED ARBITRARY BASES

Although the three main bases for expressing test scores are sufficient to account for most commonly used scores, there are still a few which are unique. We shall mention several very briefly.

Type IV A: Nonmeaningful Scaled Scores

Several publishers use scaled scores which are nonmeaningful in themselves, but which are extremely useful in giving a common basis for equating different forms and/or levels of a test. The previously mentioned *CEEB*-score, as used today, has many elements of such a scaled score. *CEEB*-scores originally were linear standard scores with a mean of 500 and a standard deviation of 100; however, for more than twenty years the results of each year's edition have been keyed statistically to the 1941 results. Thus, these *CEEB*-scores are not directly interpretable for today's examinees, and percentile ranks are used for that purpose.

We shall consider only one more example: the *SCAT*-scale developed by the Educational Testing Service. This is a nonmeaningful scaled score used with its *School and College Abilities Tests* (SCAT) and its *Sequential Tests of Educational Progress* (STEP). ETS sought deliberately a scale using numbers that would not be confused with scores from other scales. The scale was constructed so that a scaled score of 300 would equal a percentage-correct score of 60, and a scaled score of 260, a percentage-correct score of 20. These scaled score values are used as a statistical convenience for the publisher, but percentile bands are used for interpreting results.

Type IV B: Long-Range Equi-Unit Scales

None of the scores mentioned has a scale of equal units except within a narrow range or under certain assumptions. For some purposes, it is most desirable to have a single equi-unit scale covering a wide span of ages.

An early attempt at constructing such a scale resulted in the *T*-score and *T*-scaled score, mentioned earlier. As originally conceived by McCall, this scale was to use 50 for the mean of an unselected group of twelve-year-olds. The mean for older groups would be higher, for younger groups lower. The standard deviation would be 10 at all age levels.

Another early attempt was made by Heinis, who developed mental growth units which he believed were more nearly uniform in size than mental age units. These, in turn, were made to yield a Personal Constant which he felt was more consistent than the IQ over a period of years. Although Kuhlmann-Anderson norms have used the PC, they have never been widely accepted.

A present-day example of such a scale is the *K-score* scales developed by Gardner. The average score of tenth-graders is set at 100, and the unit of measurement is set at one-seventh the standard deviation of fifth-graders. The rationale underlying the scale is too complex to go into here, but it has been applied to the *Stanford Achievement Tests* (published by Harcourt, Brace & World, Inc.).

The principal advantage of such long-range equi-unit scales is to be found in various research applications. For the most part, they do not lend themselves well to direct interpretation. Their underlying rationale is usually involved and their development complicated. The reader who is interested in such scores may obtain further information from any of the more technical measurements references.

Type IV C: Deviation IQ (Otis-style)

It is fitting, perhaps, to come to the end of our long succession of scores with another IQ—the fourth one that we have mentioned. (Is it any wonder that the IQ is a confusing score?)

The deviation IQ as used on *Otis* intelligence tests and certain others is basically different from the Type II deviation IQ's. In the development of the Otis-style deviation IQ, a norm (or average) is found for each of several age groups. We obtain an examinee's IQ by finding his raw score, subtracting his age norm, and adding 100; the result shows an examinee's deviation from his age norm in raw-score units.

FORMULA:

$$(\text{Otis}) \; IQ = 100 + (X - \overline{X}_{\text{age norm}}), \text{ where}$$

X = any person's raw score on an Otis intelligence test

$\overline{X}_{\text{age norm}}$ = average raw score for those in the norm group whose chronological age is the same as the examinee's.

This deviation IQ has a mean of 100, but the standard deviation is not controlled as were the standard deviations of the Type II deviation IQ's. Because of this, the standard deviations of Otis-style IQ's may vary from age to age and make interpretations difficult.

A FINAL WORD

We have considered many types of test score in this chapter. With only one or two exceptions, they are all in widespread use. The personnel worker in industry is likely to encounter relatively few of them—probably only Types II A and II B (interindividual comparisons considering mean and standard deviation, and considering rank within group). The school teacher or the guidance worker may very well encounter any of them.

Test scores would be much easier to interpret—for all of us, experts and novices alike—if only we could agree upon a single type of score, or even on just a few.

Considering all factors, I should like to see the day when we would use only percentile ranks or percentile bands in test interpretation. This score has limitations, to be sure—all scores do. But the score has some inherent meaning and is easy for the layman to grasp. With a single type of score, we could direct our attention to educating everyone to its meaning and to its principal limitation, the difference in distances between various percentile points. We could stress, too, the importance of knowing the composition of the norm group (or groups).

There is little question but what percentile ranks can do everything that the IQ can, regardless of which of the four types we use. And percentile ranks within grade or within age have many advantages over grade-placement and age scores.

We might still have need for special warning about the use of percentile ranks on very short tests where the difference of a single raw-score value may mean a great difference in percentile rank, but the percentile band, of course, is a protection here. And we still have need for other kinds of scores for research, because percentile ranks do not lend themselves well to mathematical manipulation; indeed, we cannot even average them.

We must remember that a test score must be understood before it can be interpreted. And it would be easier to learn one score thoroughly than to try to learn something about many assorted scores.

Even more important than any of these considerations, of course, is the quality of the test itself. I cannot emphasize too strongly that the quality of the test itself is more important than anything else! A poor test is still a poor test even if it has fine printing, elaborate norms tables, and a wealth of statistical work-ups. A good test is one which will do the job we want it to, will do so consistently, and will possess those practical features (such as cost, time required, etc.) which make it usable for our purposes.

Test scores are used to express test performance. If they permit us to understand more about how well a person has done on a test, they are better scores than those which obscure such understanding. But no score can be meaningful if the test is poor in quality or lacks validity or has low reliability. And, although derived scores can be more meaningful than raw scores, they cannot be more accurate.

For More Information

Two aids to a better understanding of the scores described in this chapter may be found in the Appendix. Table 10 is essentially a summary of each of the scores, listing for each type of score: its rationale, advantages, limitations, and (where appropriate) a formula. Table 9 is a conversion table, permitting translation among all Type II A and II B scores—under the assumption of a normal probability distribution.

Chapter Seven

PROFILES

There is a map-maker, I hear, who deliberately draws some non-existent feature—perhaps a tiny village, a lake, or a stream—on each of his maps in an effort to trap any would-be copier. The place of course does not exist after it appears on the map any more than it did before appearing there. A good map reflects features which exist in reality, but it does not make their existence any more real or any less real.

In exactly the same way, a test *profile* (sometimes called *psychograph*) portrays the test scores of an individual. The profile is a graphic device enabling us to see the over-all performance of an individual at a glance. An important point to remember, though, is that the profile does not make the scores any more true. Most of us find it surprisingly easy to believe that a score must be accurate if we have seen it on a test profile. And most of us find it especially easy to see apparent differences in score as being real differences. We need to remind ourselves that the differences are not necessarily significant just because they are some distance apart on the profile form.

Profiles are a convenient way of showing test scores. They provide an excellent means for gaining an over-all picture of a person's strengths and weaknesses. Profiles can be very helpful provided we use suitable caution in their interpretation.

In general, a profile is used only when we wish to show two or more scores for the same person. These scores may be based on parts of the same test or of the same test battery—or they may be based on different tests entirely. In this latter instance, we should be especially careful when using the same profile sheet for tests with distinctly different norm groups. Any observed difference in score is likely to be more a function of the different norm groups than of any real difference in aptitude, achievement, etc.

Profiles show the test variable along one axis of the graph and show the score values along the other axis. Profile forms may show score values along the vertical axis or along the horizontal; there is no particular reason for preferring the one over the other so far as ease of reading is concerned. If we have to prepare our own profile sheets, we will probably want to list our test variables down the left-hand side of the sheet and to plot our scores along the horizontal axis of the profile. We do this because it is easier to write the complete test identification along a line than to write it within the narrow confines of a column.

SPECIFIC-TEST PROFILES

There are two basic types of profile. The first is prepared by the test publisher for a *specific* test or test battery; the second is a *general* profile form which may be used for almost any test.

Figure 14 shows a profile for Sam Sweeney who has taken the *Kuder Preference Record: Vocational (Form C)*. This form has been designed so that the examinee may construct his own profile. His raw scores for each of the several interest areas are entered at the top of the respective columns. The examinee locates each score in the half of the column labelled "M" (for his sex), and draws a line across the column. By blackening the entire column beneath that line, he has constructed a bar graph showing his relative preference for activities in these ten vocational areas as defined by Kuder. Sam's percentile rank for each area may be read along the calibration at either side of the graph. Note how the percentiles "bunch up" around 50—just as we would expect from our knowledge of the normal curve.

Sam is a twenty-four-year-old male who, having completed his military service, is now a college junior. He is interested in science and thinks that he might like college teaching. There is nothing in this profile to suggest that this would be an unwise choice. We might have urged caution if he had indicated high interest in

NAME *SWEENEY, SAM* *S.* AGE *24* SEX *M* GROUP *MEN* DATE OF TEST *10/10/62*
Print Last First Initial M or F

First Revision, February 1951
REPRODUCTION BY ANY MEANS STRICTLY PROHIBITED

PROFILE SHEET

for the

KUDER PREFERENCE RECORD
VOCATIONAL

Forms CH, CM

MEN and WOMEN

DIRECTIONS FOR PROFILING

1. Copy the V-Score from the back page of your answer pad in the box at the right.

41

If your V-Score is 37 or less, there is some reason for doubting the value of your answers, and your other scores may not be very accurate. *If your V-Score is 45 or more,* you may not have understood the directions, since 44 is the highest possible score. *If your score is not between 38 and 44,* inclusive, you should see your adviser. He will probably recommend that you read the directions again, and then that you fill out the blank a second time, being careful to follow the directions exactly and to give sincere replies.

If your V-Score is between 38 and 44, inclusive, go ahead with the following directions.

2. Copy the scores 0 through 9 in the spaces at the top of the profile chart. Under "OUTDOOR" find the number which is the same as the score at the top. If your score is not shown, draw a line *between* the scores above and below your own. Use the numbers under M if you are a man and the numbers under F if you are a woman. Draw a line through this number from one side to the other of the entire column under OUTDOOR. Do the same thing for the scores at the top of each of the other columns. If a score is larger than any number in the column, draw a line across the top of the column; if it is smaller, draw a line across the bottom.

3. With your pencil blacken the entire space between the lines you have drawn and the bottom of the chart. The result is your profile for the *Kuder Preference Record—Vocational.*

An interpretation of the scores will be found on the other side.

Published by Science Research Associates, Inc.
259 East Erie Street, Chicago 11, Illinois

Copyright ©1951, by G. Frederic Kuder. Copyright under International Copyright Union. All rights reserved. Printed in the U.S.A.

SRA Catalog Number 7-299

(Reprinted by permission.)

Figure 14.

Artistic or Musical and low in Scientific and Persuasive. We would still need additional information of course before offering positive encouragement. What sort of ability does he have? What are his grades?

A somewhat different use of the bar graph approach to showing test results is found in Figure 15, representing Grace Gibbs' performance on the *Differential Aptitude Tests*. Although the vertical axis again shows percentile ranks, the bars here are drawn out from the median; the publisher, The Psychological Corporation, prefers to emphasize deviation from the average in this manner. National norms for eleventh-grade girls were used.

This profile sheet is taken from a six-page interpretive folder, "Your Aptitudes as measured by the *Differential Aptitude Tests*." Here again the percentile points are closer together near 50, as they should be. An important feature of this profile sheet is the discussion of "important differences" directly below the profile; note, however, that the original page size is larger than that shown here. Other pages in this student folder describe the meaning of aptitude and of the test areas of the *Differential Aptitude Tests*. In addition, one whole page is devoted to "How Much Confidence Can Be Placed in Tests?", and includes an excellent discussion of expectancy tables.

This case, adapted from a casebook for the DAT published by The Psychological Corporation, concerns an eleventh-grade student of about average ability who was failing in her school's commercial curriculum. After counseling, Grace decided to transfer to a dressmaking course, thereby presumably capitalizing on her above-average ability in Space Relations and Mechanical Reasoning. In this new curriculum, Grace's attitude toward school improved, her grades picked up, and she graduated from high school the following year.

There was reason to believe that Grace had fooled herself into thinking that she wanted commercial work. Her highest scores on a vocational interest test were Computational and Clerical. She was sufficiently mature, however, to discuss her problem with her school counselor and to act on sensible advice. Also helpful here was the fact that her parents were cooperative and did not object to Grace's change to a lower-status objective.

A third bar-graph approach is found in Figure 16, showing Nancy

Profiling Your DAT Scores

The numbers that tell how you did on each test are in the row marked "Percentiles." Your percentile tells where you rank on a test in comparison with boys or girls in your grade. These percentiles are based on test scores earned by thousands of students in numerous schools across the country. If your percentile rank is 50, you are just in the middle — that is, one-half of the students in the national group did better than you and one-half did less well. (If your school uses local norms, your counselor will explain the difference.)

In the columns below each percentile you can draw your aptitude profile. For each test make a *heavy short line* across the column at the level which corresponds to your percentile rank on that test.

Your aptitude profile will be more visible if you black in each column *up to* or *down to* the 50-line from the short lines you have just made. The vertical bars on your profile show the strength of your tested aptitudes, *up* or *down* from the rank of the *middle student* of your grade and sex.

More about Percentiles

Think of "percentile" as meaning "per cent of people." In your case, the people are boys or girls in your grade in many schools across the country. The percentile shows what per cent of this group scored no higher than you did. If your percentile rank on one test is 80, you are at the top of 80 per cent of the group —only 20 per cent made higher scores than yours. If you scored in the 25th percentile, this would mean about 75 per cent of the group did better than you on the test. Thus, a percentile rank always indicates your relative standing among a theoretical 100 persons representing a large "norm" group — in this case, students of your sex and grade. It does NOT tell how many questions (or what per cent of them) you answered correctly.

Note

If your teacher gives you a label with your name, raw scores, and percentiles on it, first peel off the backing and expose the sticky surface. Then place it carefully so that the percentile numbers are just above the columns in the chart, and press it down firmly.

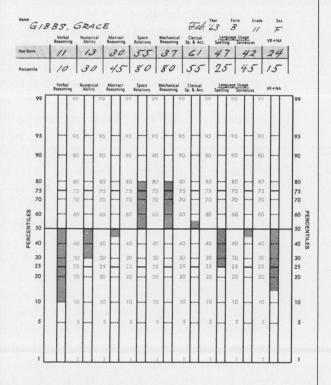

Name GIBBS, GRACE					Year Feb.'63	Form B	Grade 11	Sex F

	Verbal Reasoning	Numerical Ability	Abstract Reasoning	Space Relations	Mechanical Reasoning	Clerical Sp. & Acc.	Language Usage Spelling	Sentences	VR+NA
Raw Score	11	13	30	55	37	61	47	42	24
Percentile	10	30	45	80	80	55	25	45	15

How Big a Difference Is Important?

Of course we do not want to over-estimate small differences in ability on tests because a test cannot be perfectly accurate, and your score might not be exactly the same if you could take the same test twice.

To estimate the importance of a difference between your scores on any two tests on this profile, use a ruler to measure how much higher on the chart one mark is than the other. It is the *vertical* distance ↑ that counts, of course, *not* how far *across* the chart ╱ or ╲ .

If the distance is *one inch or greater*,* it is probable that you have a real difference in your abilities on the two tests.

If a difference between the two percentile ranks is *between a half inch and one inch,* consider whether other things you know about yourself agree with it; the difference may or may not be important.

If the vertical distance between two tests is *less than a half inch,* the difference between the two scores may be disregarded; so small a difference is probably not meaningful.

Copyright, 1961, The Psychological Corporation, New York 17, N. Y. (Reprinted by permission.)

*On the original form (which is larger than this reproduction).

Figure 15.

Namyl's scores on the *Metropolitan Achievement Tests (Elementary)*. Once again, the bars are drawn out from the median. This time, though, the bars are drawn horizontally and the stanine scores are plotted. Note that grade-equivalent (grade-placement) and standard scores are also shown.

Nancy's case, adapted from one presented by World Book Company (now, Harcourt, Brace & World, Inc.), illustrates the value of an achievement battery in the elementary grades. Nancy is a nine-year-old just starting the fourth grade. Her grades last year were uniformly good—all A's and B's. This battery, though, suggests that last year's teacher may have overlooked Nancy's arithmetic. She seems to have a specific deficiency here. Notice that her Arithmetic Problem Solving, although low, appears distinctly higher than her Arithmetic Computation; apparently, she is able to use her very high reading ability effectively in solving some of the problems. Essentially, this battery has confirmed Nancy's high over-all ability and has directed attention to an area in which Nancy may need some extra help.

Figure 17 shows a different kind of profile—this time, a line graph. The information shown of course is similar; however, this approach directs attention to the relationship between some of the subtests. Note that every value plotted on the profile is based on at least twenty-five items; with rare exceptions should separate scores be based on fewer items than this. The figure shows Will Warren's results on the California Test Bureau's *Multiple Aptitude Tests*. Note the statement about the significance of differences between scores.

Will is a fifteen-year-old ninth-grader who plans to go to college. At present, he is interested in both the physical and social sciences, and has also considered engineering. On the basis of these results, we could assure Will that he has sufficient potential for college work. We might advise him to continue thinking about college and about different occupations. His relatively low scores in Spatial Visualization suggest that he may be wise to consider occupations other than engineering, but we may decide to wait for another year or two before stressing any negative implication these scores may have for engineering. We might want to stress that good grades are also important for any student who wants to go to a first-class college.

Figure 18 is a profile of Dorothy Darley's scores on two different administrations of the *Iowa Tests of Basic Skills*. This profile, by the

Metropolitan Achievement Tests

INDIVIDUAL PROFILE CHART / ELEMENTARY BATTERY

NAME _NAMYL_   _NANCY_   _N._   BOY ☐   GIRL ☒
     Last   First   Initial

GRADE PLACEMENT _4.1_ TEACHER _Miss Keyes_ SCHOOL _Clifton Elem._

DATE OF TESTING _Oct. 7, 1962_ DATE OF BIRTH _July 5, 1953_ AGE _9 – 3_
                                                          Yrs.   Mos.

FORM OF TEST USED _B_   NORMS: NATIONAL ☑ for _4.1_
                                      LOCAL ☐   Time

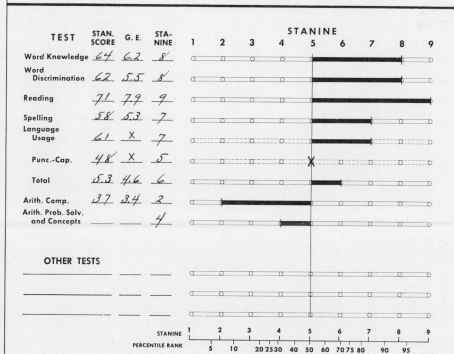

TEST	STAN. SCORE	G.E.	STA-NINE
Word Knowledge	64	6.2	8
Word Discrimination	62	5.5	8
Reading	71	7.9	9
Spelling	58	5.3	7
Language Usage	61	X	7
Punc.-Cap.	48	X	5
Total	5.3	4.6	6
Arith. Comp.	37	3.4	2
Arith. Prob. Solv. and Concepts	—	—	4

OTHER TESTS

STANINE   1   2   3   4   5   6   7   8   9

PERCENTILE RANK   5   10   20 25 30   40   50   60   70 75 80   90   95

Figure 16.

Figure 17.

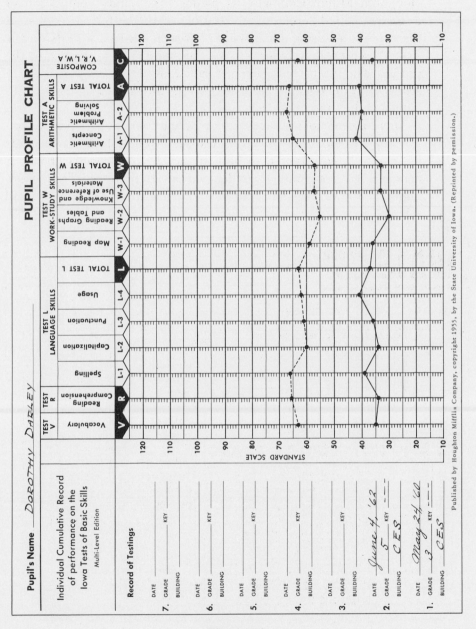

Figure 18.

145

Houghton Mifflin Company, is planned for handy comparison of as many as six different administrations of the battery. It does so at the expense of using small spaces between successive units on the scale of scores, thereby effectively flattening the appearance of the profile. The units used here, incidentally, are grade-placement scores with the decimal points removed; thus, 35 means 3.5, or fifth month of the third grade, etc.

There are obvious advantages to having two or more administrations of a test battery drawn on the same profile form. If the tests are carefully constructed to be comparable (the specific items, of course, differ from grade to grade), we can study the child's progress. Dorothy shows excellent progress, having increased her over-all

WAIS RECORD FORM
Wechsler Adult Intelligence Scale

Name _MONA MANLEY_
Birth Date _2/10/17_ Age _46_ Sex _F_ Marital: S M D Ⓦ
Nat. _U.S._ Color _WHITE_ Tested by _HBL_
Place of Examination _OFFICE — U.C._ Date _3/10/63_
Occupation _NEWS REPORTER_ Education _1 YR. GRADUATE WORK_

TABLE OF SCALED SCORE EQUIVALENTS*

RAW SCORE

Scaled Score	Information	Comprehension	Arithmetic	Similarities	Digit Span	Vocabulary	Digit Symbol	Picture Completion	Block Design	Picture Arrangement	Object Assembly	Scaled Score
19	29	27-28		26	17	78-80	87-90					19
18	28	26		25		76-77	83-86	21		36	44	18
17	27	25	18	24		74-75	79-82		48	35	43	17
16	26	24	17	23	16	71-73	76-78	20	47	34	42	16
15	25	23	16	22	15	67-70	72-75		46	33	41	15
14	23-24	22	15	21	14	63-66	69-71	19	44-45	32	40	14
13	21-22	21	14	19-20		59-62	66-68	18	42-43	30-31	38-39	13
12	19-20	20	13	17-18	13	54-58	62-65	17	39-41	28-29	36-37	12
11	17-18	19	12	15-16	12	47-53	58-61	15-16	35-38	26-27	34-35	11
10	15-16	17-18	11	13-14	11	40-46	52-57	14	31-34	23-25	31-33	10
9	13-14	15-16	10	12	10	32-39	47-51	12-13	28-30	20-22	28-30	9
8	11-12	14	9	9-10		26-31	41-46	10-11	26-27	18-19	25-27	8
7	9-10	12-13	7-8	7-8	9	22-25	35-40	8-9	21-24	15-17	22-24	7
6	7-8	10-11	6	5-6	8	18-21	29-34	6-7	17-20	12-14	19-21	6
5	5-6	8-9	5	4		14-17	23-28	5	13-16	9-11	15-18	5
4	4	6-7	4	3	7	11-13	18-22	4	10-12	8	11-14	4
3	3	5	3	2		10	15-17	3	6-9	7	8-10	3
2	2	4	2	1	6	9	13-14	2	3-5	6	5-7	2
1	1	3	1		4-5	8	12	1	2	5	3-4	1
0	0	0-2	0	0	0-3	0-7	0-11	0	0-1	0-4	0-2	0

SUMMARY

TEST	Raw Score	Scaled Score	
Information	26	16	
Comprehension	23	15	
Arithmetic	14	13	
Similarities	9	8	
Digit Span	14	14	
Vocabulary	72	16	
Verbal Score			82
Digit Symbol	74	15	
Picture Completion	19	14	
Block Design	29	9	
Picture Arrangement	18	8	
Object Assembly	33	10	
Performance Score			56
Total Score			138

VERBAL SCORE _82_ IQ _124_
PERFORMANCE SCORE _56_ IQ _120_
FULL SCALE SCORE _138_ IQ _123_

*Clinicians who wish to draw a "psychograph" on the above table may do so by connecting the subject's raw scores. The interpretation of any such profile, however, should take into account the reliabilities of the subtests and the lower reliabilities of *differences between subtest scores.*

The Psychological Corporation, New York, N. Y., copyright 1947, © 1955. (Reprinted by permission.)

Figure 19.

score by 2.8 grade-equivalents in two years. In Reading Comprehension her improvement is 3.2 grade-equivalents. Probably the most important point to note is that Dorothy now tends to score somewhat above her actual grade placement whereas only two years ago she tested at or very slightly below her grade placement. It will be interesting to see whether Dorothy retains her increased achievement rate when retested in another two years; there seems to be a promise in the second testing that was not evident in the first.

Another sort of profile is shown in Figure 19, the *Wechsler Adult Intelligence Scale* results for Mona Manley. The WAIS is an individual test of intelligence published by The Psychological Corporation. The profile is obtained as a by-product in getting the scaled scores necessary for computing the IQ's. Some psychologists, however, have tried to use it as a personality test by noting relative peaks and dips—despite the publisher's warning at the bottom of the profile.

Mrs. Manley is a forty-six-year-old widow who is receiving psychotherapy from a clinical psychologist. Her WAIS results indicate high average intelligence and may suggest something as to the nature of her present difficulties. Skilled clinicians can obtain additional clues from such individual tests by observing the counselee's behavior, noting unusual responses, etc.

Test profiles that may be shown to examinees (or to parents) should show clearly the titles of the various tests; however, personality tests are an exception to that principle—especially if any of the variables might be construed as threatening by the examinee. Figure 20 shows a profile of David Dyman's scores on the *California Psychological Inventory* (published by the Consulting Psychologists Press, Inc.). Note that the titles of the scales are given only in abbreviated form—meaningful to the test user, but not to the examinee. The breaks in the profile call attention to the four classes of measures found with the CPI: (1) measures of poise, ascendancy, and self-assurance; (2) measures of socialization, maturity, and responsibility; (3) measures of achievement potential and intellectual efficiency; and (4) measures of intellectual and interest modes. *T*-score values are the derived scores shown at the left and right in the profile.

David Dyman, a case adapted from the *CPI Manual* (with permission of the publisher, the Consulting Psychologists Press, Inc.) is a seventeen-year-old high school student named by his principal

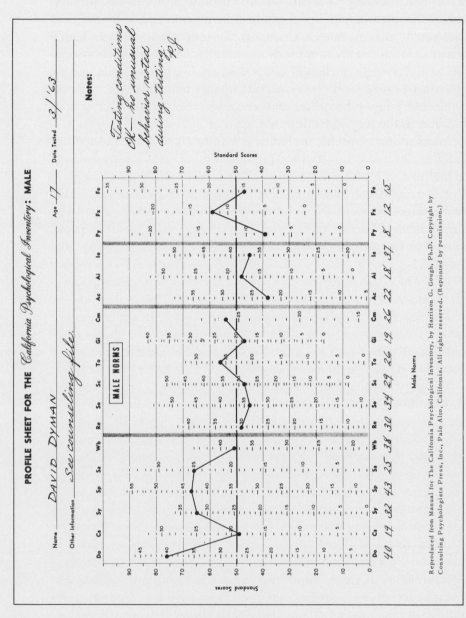

Figure 20.

as an outstanding student leader. Although he ranks high in scholastic aptitude, his achievement had been only average. The test profile is high for the Class I measures, especially Do (Dominance). Most other scores are near average (50) and would be difficult to interpret meaningfully. Of some interest, though, is the low Ac (Achievement) score which suggests that the boy's academic achievement may be below what would be expected of him considering his ability, drive, etc.

Profiles are especially useful when it may be desirable to consider relative scores or the interaction of scores on several scales of a test.

We could go on almost endlessly noting additional profiles, each indicating something just a bit different from the others. But let us finish this particular section with just two more profiles. These, shown in Figures 21 and 22, illustrate Branch Baxter's performance on the *Sequential Tests of Educational Progress* (STEP) and the *School and College Ability Tests* (SCAT). The profiles are adapted from cases presented in manuals prepared by the publisher, the Educational Testing Service, and are used here with their permission.

Figure 21 shows Branch's profiles on the STEP and SCAT as they would appear in the guidance file at his school. On the original form, STEP and SCAT profiles are on different sides of the sheet, and instructions for interpretation are included. (The form is modified here for easier presentation on a single sheet.) Figure 22 shows the same scores on a special individual report sheet which might be given to either Branch or his parents. ETS focuses our attention immediately on the fact that test scores are approximate by creating a percentile band (by shading a range of scores). This percentile band extends from approximately one standard error below an obtained score to approximately one standard error above the score. This approach is commendable, for it minimizes the likelihood of gross misinterpretation when it directs attention to the error of measurement. If the bands for two scores overlap (as, for example, Social Studies and Writing, and Mathematics and Science), the difference in score is probably inconsequential; however, if the two bands do not overlap, we may have some confidence that the obtained difference is not merely a chance difference.

Branch is a high school junior, sixteen years of age, who hopes to

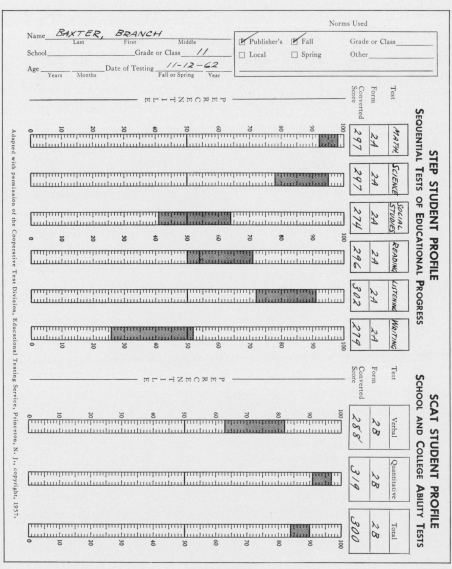

Figure 21.

major in theoretical physics in college. His Mathematics (especially), Science, and Listening scores are high. In his Social Studies and Writing tests, he is only about average when compared with other eleventh-graders nationally. On Reading, he is slightly above average. On the SCAT, his Quantitative score is very high; his Verbal score, though above average for high school juniors, is significantly lower than the Quantitative. His high scores fit his present vocational goals. If his course grades are in line with his test scores, he should have little difficulty in getting into a good college. If I were Branch's counselor, I would encourage him to devote some effort during his senior year to developing greater competence in social studies and writing, perhaps noting the relevance of such skills to the work of the physicist.

Figure 22 shows exactly the same results as Figure 21, but is designed to be read by the student or his parents. Once again the percentile bands are used, and the student is encouraged to think of the others who fall within that band as having received the same score he did. This page is part of a four-page folder designed to be given to the student and his parents. The folder contains a description of the tests and a statement about the significance of differences in score.

GENERAL PROFILES

The greatest advantage of general profile forms is that several different tests may be shown on the same sheet. The greatest limitation of such forms is the ease with which we may put tests with drastically dissimilar norm groups on the same sheet.

Figure 23 is an example of a good general profile form, for it has both a percentile scale and a standard-score scale and calls for: title and form of the test, the norm group, the raw score, two different derived scores, and the date of testing. When preparing such a profile we should be careful to give complete information on all tests. What seems self-evident at the moment of recording may not be so obvious months later.

We need to be especially careful to record a complete designation of the norm group. My personal feeling is that it is best not to draw the profile for any test which has norms very much different from

Figure 22.

Figure 23. Test Record and Profile Chart.

153

those for the other tests shown. In any event, we should never draw lines connecting scores from completely separate tests—unless, of course, the same norm group has been used in standardizing the different tests (as with the *Differential Aptitude Tests,* the *Sequential Tests of Educational Progress,* etc.).

The Good Profile

What then may we say about the characteristics of a good profile form? One way or another, there must be full information about the test: title, form, level, etc. There must be no ambiguity as to the nature of norm group used. The examinee's name should appear along with other appropriate identifying information. The date or dates of testing must be indicated. The examiner's name may be important, especially if an individual test is involved. If there was any deviation in testing conditions (as, for example, when the test's time limits are altered, either deliberately or accidentally), this fact should be noted, too.

A good profile form should be designed so that the derived-score scale is appropriate. If it shows percentile ranks, the scale should be drawn so that units near the median are much smaller than units near the extremes. In other words, the scale should be drawn in accordance with the properties of the normal probability curve. (The need for this is not so great when percentile bands are used— as in the case of the STEP and the SCAT shown in Figures 21 and 22—for the bands themselves call attention to the standard error of measurement.) The use of several derived scores may be very helpful, as we saw in Figure 16.

Clear directions for the preparation of the profile should accompany the form; if feasible, the directions should be printed on the form itself. A clear and precise statement of the types of scores used should also accompany the profile, preferably printed on the form itself. The composition of the norm group should be explained fully in material accompanying the profile. If there are several norm groups which can be used, there should be space on the form for indicating which group is being used.

The Raw Score

We should be certain to record the raw score (or its equivalent nonmeaningful scaled score) for every test variable in the profile. In the first place, it should be there so that we may check the profile plots. Mistakes are more likely to be made in plotting profile points than in copying raw scores from one sheet to another. If the raw scores appear on the profile sheet, we are more likely to check the accuracy of the plots.

Then, too, the presence of the raw scores makes it easier for us to compare the examinee with another norm group.

> Janie's profile showed her scores when compared with a group of applicants. I wanted to compare her with employees, as well. Since the raw score for each test variable was appropriately recorded on the profile, I was able to obtain this additional information with a minimum of work.

The presence of the raw scores also facilitates research, either formal or informal. The counselor who develops a hunch that a certain subgroup is different from some other subgroup can make a quick preliminary check from the raw scores readily available to him. As we have noted before, raw scores are better for research than most derived scores—much better, of course, than percentile ranks.

Difference in Profile Points

How far apart must scores be before we can be sure that they are really different? It all depends.

If the norm groups used for the two (or more) test variables are not the same, we probably cannot say; certainly we cannot say unless the groups are truly comparable. Whether we like it or not, this is the case. No amount of rationalization can justify our comparing scores on two tests when the norm groups are markedly different.

If the scores are not reported in the same units, we cannot say—at least not until we convert them to the same type of score unit.

We have noted several times that no score is perfectly accurate. Every test score includes some amount of error. If a person were to take a large number of comparable forms of the same test, his score would vary somewhat from form to form even if the forms were designed to give identical results on the average. We found in Chapter Four that the standard error of measurement is an estimate of what the standard deviation of an individual's scores would be if he were to take these many forms.

When two tests are involved, both scores are subject to measurement error and we must consider both measurement errors. We can be very certain that a given difference represents a real difference (that is, one caused not just by the unreliability of the scores) if bands extending out two standard errors of measurement from each score do not overlap.

> For example, Pat obtains T-scores of 76 and 65 on two different tests of the same aptitude battery. Let us assume that the SE_{meas} for each test is 2.0. We may be about 95 per cent confident that Pat's true score on the first test is between 72 and 80 (i.e., 76 ± 2 SE's) and that her true score on the second test is between 61 and 69 (i.e., 65 ± 4). Since there is no overlap between 72-80 and 61-69, we may be highly certain that the observed difference is in the true direction; in other words, we may be reasonably certain that Pat has more of the first aptitude than of the second.

This is a more rigorous standard, however, than we need to use. We can estimate the SE of measurement of a difference through the use of the formula:

$$SE_{\text{diff meas}} = \sqrt{SE^2_{\text{meas }x} + SE^2_{\text{meas }y}} \text{ , where}$$

$SE_{\text{meas }x}$ = standard error of measurement on Test X.
$SE_{\text{meas }y}$ = standard error of measurement on Test Y.

> Using this statistic on Pat's scores, we would find that the $SE_{\text{diff meas}} = \sqrt{2^2 + 2^2} = \sqrt{8} = 2.83$. If we apply this statistic, we would conclude that any difference between the two aptitude tests that was greater than two $SE_{\text{diff meas}}$ (here, 2×2.83, or 5.66) would not be reasonably attributed to chance. Since there is a difference of 11 between Pat's scores, we would conclude that she was really higher on the first test than the second.

But neither of these methods considers the extent of correlation between the two tests. It can be shown that the reliability of a difference in scores is a function of the reliability of the two tests and the correlation between them. If the correlation between two tests is high, both are measuring much the same thing; therefore, more differences will be only chance differences. Several people have used these facts in developing still other approaches to the study of significance of differences between scores.

At the present time, there is no completely satisfactory way of deciding definitely how big a difference in score must be before it can be considered a true difference. Therefore it seems best to follow the suggestions contained in the test manual or on the test profile. We should, however, study the manual carefully to determine what rationale the publisher is using.

Where the manual for the multiple-score test or test battery suggests no method for determining real differences between scores, I use the $SE_{diff\ meas}$. This formula is easy to employ if the manual includes standard errors of measurement for the different tests—and it usually does. In fact, more and more publishers are including some procedure for determining which differences are probably real ones.

The significance of differences between scores is presently receiving considerable attention among professional measurements people. Probably more than half of the total literature on the problem has appeared within the last five or six years. We may hope to have a better understanding of the whole topic and much more general agreement within the next few years.

Profile Analysis

When there are several scores reported for an individual (as in a profile), we may be tempted to try a profile analysis—that is, we may try to find additional meaning through the relative peaks and dips. On the *Wechsler Adult Intelligence Scale*, for example, some clinical psychologists believe that relationships between scores on certain of the eleven scales can be used as a basis for personality diagnosis. Research, however, has not resulted in much clear-cut evidence that such diagnoses are meaningful.

Nevertheless research on profile analysis continues with further study of the WAIS and other multiple-scale tests. The authors of the California Test Bureau's *Multiple Aptitude Tests* have prepared a number of typical profiles of occupational and other groups, suggesting that an examinee's profile may be compared with these examples Gough proposes certain interpretations for various combinations of scores on his *California Psychological Inventory* (Consulting Psychologists Press).

We should remember that any sort of profile analysis depends upon the reliability of two or more tests, and we need to be very cautious. Some of these approaches may be promising, but we should examine their research basis carefully before using them.

Please note that there are many circumstances in which scores may be used jointly to obtain better prediction of criterion values than can be obtained through the use of any one variable by itself; however, this topic (multiple correlation and multiple regression) is beyond the scope of this book.

Chapter Eight

COMMON
SENSE

When test results do not make sense, the test results may be wrong—or our "common sense" may be faulty. Neither is perfect.

Any testing program should call for checking at every stage where mistakes are possible. As test users, we should be prepared to check the scores that are put into our hands. If the test results do not seem reasonable, they may be wrong; on the other hand, our expectations may have been in error and the tests may be right.

> Several years ago I was looking over a multiple-score test taken by a college student as part of a campus-wide testing program. I was surprised that this good student had no scores above the median. Upon checking, I discovered that one of the scoring clerks had not understood the directions for using the norms table. She had taken raw-score values from the test, entered these in the percentile-ranks column, and read out the corresponding entries in the raw-score column as percentile ranks. Since there had been no system of checking results, more than 1,000 test sheets and profiles had to be re-examined.

On the other hand:

> A company was testing several people for a junior-level management position. Al Athol had been an employee of the company for several years, had a good work history, and was well-liked by fellow employees and by management. The other candidates were very recent college graduates and new to the firm. Al did as well

159

as the other candidates except on a spatial relations test; on this, he did very poorly. The personnel director decided to select one of the other men because of this one very low score—and it is doubtful whether spatial relations skill is even involved in the management position! This personnel director should have used a little common sense, for Al was clearly superior to the other men on the various nontest factors that should have been considered.

When test results and common sense seem to be in conflict, we need to check all possibilities. There are four: (1) tests may be wrong; (2) common sense may be wrong; (3) both may be wrong; and (4) neither may be wrong.

Later in this chapter we shall deal at some length with common mistakes in testing. For the moment, let us see how common sense can be wrong. Are we sure that our preconceptions are correct? Is this really an able man, or has he succeeded by saying the right thing at the right time? Is this student really good or is he an "apple polisher"? Are these tests as valid for this purpose as they should be? What makes these test results seems unreasonable?

Often we may find that questioning the results will help us find errors in both our reasoning and the results. In such situations, checking really pays off—for it enables us to obtain a better understanding of the entire situation than we had before.

What about those situations, though, where test results seem unreasonable, and yet both our reasoning and the test results seem correct even after checking? In such situations we should probably stop to consider whether there is really a discrepancy between the two. Closer scrutiny may prove that the tests are giving us just a slightly different slant than the one we had been considering. Or perhaps the discrepancy is not so great as we had thought at first. If these lines of reasoning fail to resolve the discrepancy, we may want to get further information from tests, interviews, etc., provided that the situation is important enough to justify it.

Decision-Making

As mentioned earlier, Cronbach and Gleser, in their *Psychological Tests and Personnel Decisions,* point out that test scores often are used as one basis for making decisions. Tests are especially helpful, they note, when used in connection with institutional decisions about personnel, for here there is a backlog of information from similar situations in the past, and the expectation is that many similar decisions will have to be made in the future. The institution is not likely to be hurt badly by any single bad decision about the selection or rejection or classification of any individual. And tests, in their place, can provide information that may increase the accuracy of prediction in the long run. Common examples include: selection of students or employees, classification of personnel, etc.

Individual decisions, on the other hand, cannot be evaluated in the long run. Any specified individual is not likely to have to make this same sort of decision again. And the choice that the individual makes right now may very well have a long-lasting effect on his life. Test information, though sometimes helpful, can nowhere be *so* helpful as in institutional decisions. These individual decisions are important to the person and are unique to him. He has no backlog of similar situations—nor the expectation of facing similar situations in the future. Common examples include: deciding which curriculum to study, whether to attend college, which college to attend, which job to take, etc.

We can see why tests are better at helping us make institutional decisions. Even with the best of tests, we expect to make some mistakes; however, if we have reasonably valid tests we can make better personnel decisions with them than we could without them. The institution expects occasional bad personnel decisions. No particular bad decision is likely to have any lasting effect on the institution.

In contrast are the guidance and counseling situations in which tests may be used. Where the tests are considered in making individual decisions, we must be very cautious. Except in the most extreme cases, no test can tell whether a student should go to college, which type of training one should take, etc. As a general rule tests can be of most help in a negative way; that is, by ruling out certain alternatives.

Some Common Mistakes

Besides the measurement error inherent in any test, there are many possibilities of mistakes being made in the administration and scoring of a test and in reporting its results. The test user should make it part of his regular routine to check reported test scores whenever feasible.

Some sort of check should be made at every stage of testing to insure near-perfect accuracy of conditions for administration, scoring, and recording. Most of the mistakes are relatively simple things: failing to start the stopwatch used in timing; failing to stop at the proper time limit; omitting part of the directions; using the wrong answer sheet; using the wrong scoring key; lining up the scoring key incorrectly; making a mistake in counting; using a wrong scoring formula; using the wrong norms tables; reading the norms table incorrectly; misreading a handwritten score; making an error in copying, etc. Over the years I have discovered some classic mistakes. I shall pass a few of them along, partly for comic relief and partly to show that one cannot be too compulsive in checking on tests.

> One national testing program once sent me a set of the wrong tests. The tests were not to be opened until the morning of the examination, and when they were—did we have fun!
> I shall never forget the chaos created when about 500 of 1200 machine-scoring answer sheets proved to have been printed a little off center—not enough for the eye to detect, but more than enough to throw the scoring machine off. Hand-scoring a sample of answer sheets showed that something was wrong, but it took us several days to find the cause.
> I once received three successive orders of a standardized test which was printed just a bit too small; unfortunately, the scoring key was of standard size and did not match.
> Nor will I forget the time when a researcher cut off one corner of each answer sheet to keep his promise of anonymity by removing the name. This had the effect of throwing the answer sheet enough out of alignment so that the scoring machine could not get accurate scores. Our resourceful scoring-machine operator solved that one— by balancing her finger on the opposite corner, she aligned each sheet separately for the machine. Once again, the difficulty was located by noting a discrepancy when a sample of tests was pre-scored by hand.
> Errors in the scoring keys of standardized tests are rare today, for they are very carefully checked; however, errors have been known to crop up even here. There is even the story (true, I think) of several people who managed to steal a preliminary scoring key of an important test they were to take; they were caught and found guilty when they turned in perfect papers—except for the three items which had been incorrectly marked on that preliminary key.
> Have you heard about the university student who turned in a

perfect paper—many points better than anyone had ever earned before? A little checking proved that the student had been inadvertently given the check-sheet used in setting up the scoring-machine. He had merely printed his name on the sheet and turned it in. (This could not have happened if: (1) the sheet had been properly marked as a check-sheet; *or* (2) proper test security had been maintained; *or* (3) the proctors had been performing their job of watching the examinees as they marked their tests.)

Of course, I have made a few mistakes myself. At one time or another, I have: used the wrong answer sheets for a standardized test; missed a time limit while distracted by some other task; mis-scored tests by miscounting and using a wrong scoring formula, etc. I shall never forget the time that I gave a class of students the wrong course exam (I gave them one covering the next unit of study), and no student complained until the period was half over.

It is human to err, we are told. Most of these errors, though, could have been prevented. And we cannot blame the tests for mistakes like these.

Other Sources, Too!

Tests are only one source of information. And test scores are only bits of information. In any important decision, we should make full use of all of the information available to us. As information-collectors, tests do have certain advantages—most especially their objectivity. But tests are fallible instruments, and test scores are fallible bits of information.

If tests are to be used, they should contribute something. People managed to exist and to make decisions without the aid of tests for many years—and they can today. If tests provide helpful information, we should use them—if they do not, we should not! And even if we do use tests, let us not forget to consider nontest factors as well—they, too, can be important.

Chapter Nine

WHAT CAN WE SAY?

We have been concerned primarily with the task of helping test users understand the meaning of test scores. This may be sufficient for many test users, but certainly not for all.

School counselors, guidance workers, and many others have the additional problem of trying to communicate test results to all sorts of other persons. This is more involved and requires additional skill. This task is not our main concern, but it is not one that we can ignore.

No amount of reading, of course, is going to help us too much in interpreting test scores. Written admonitions are no substitute for personal experience. Even so, it is possible to learn some general principles and "tricks of the trade." Our primary emphasis in this book is directed at enabling people with limited backgrounds in psychological and educational testing to understand the nature of test scores. There is no suggestion that this book can substitute for a basic course in tests and measurements or for a course in counseling or guidance techniques. These and other courses are needed (along with practice) before a person is prepared to get full meaning from test data.

There are two main topics in this chapter: (1) *Who* is entitled to test information? and (2) *What* do we say?

WHO IS ENTITLED TO TEST INFORMATION?

As a starting point, let us agree that the examinee himself is entitled to receive information about his test results.

The Examinee

Information given to the examinee should be as detailed as is warranted by the test and as detailed as he is likely to understand. Specific scores should be given only if the examinee is also given a thorough explanation of what the scores mean and what their limitations are.

Except within the clinical-counseling or court-legal frameworks, the examinee should be told the results of his tests in as much detail as he is likely to understand; however, information should not be forced onto those who cannot assimilate it. This incident, for example, never should have happened:

> Bobby, a third-grader, was skipping down the corridor at school and chanting, "I'm a genius! I'm a genius!" Bobby did not know what the word meant, but he did know that it must be something good because his parents had been so pleased when ". . . a lady came to our house and gave me a test. And then she said, 'Why, he's a little genius!' "

Parents of Minors

In the case of minors, parents should also be told the test results —especially if they show the slightest interest or curiosity. This principle does not mean that parents should necessarily be given specific IQ's. The IQ is not an easy type of score to explain to a layman and is burdened with all sorts of false assumptions; however, percentile ranks can be understood with minimal explanation. Consider, too, some sort of percentile-band approach (see pages 112-113).

Agency Policy

School and other agencies are likely to have their own policies regarding the interpretation of test results. These policies should be made known to all people within the agency who have access to test scores, including secretaries, file clerks, and receptionists. As a rule, only professional-level workers should interpret scores to examinees, parents, or other laymen; however, in a well-run agency, there may be provision for routine release of scores to specified professional people under stated conditions. (By *professional* in this chapter, I mean to include teachers, personnel workers, and others whose positions involve working with people, but to exclude general office workers.)

Schools and Colleges

With schools and colleges, routine test results should be handled in the same way as grades and personnel files. In the event of transfer to another institution or system, these routine test results should be sent along. It is imperative that furnished test information include: date of testing, names of tests (with form, level, and edition), and raw scores; if derived scores are included, the norm groups should be identified.

On the other hand, tests given for counseling purposes (especially at the college level) should ordinarily *not* be transferred automatically. This is testing that has been done for the student's personal benefit, and test scores should not be transmitted without the permission of the student or his parents. This limitation may be modified somewhat by the specific policy of the agency and by the nature of the testing. If the counseling-purpose testing has included only an interest test or two, there is little point to obtaining permission; however, if extensive testing, especially with personality tests, is involved, the permission clearly should be obtained.

Professional Colleagues

Within any given agency (including a school system), any professional worker who has need for test data should have access to the scores. If there is reason to believe that the data are being misused, the access should be denied or withdrawn.

> Melody Meredith, a music teacher, used to drop by the counseling office toward the end of each semester and request intelligence test scores of her pupils. After a semester or two, it was noted that she was using these scores as a basis for assigning her course grades. The director of counseling spoke to her about the inadvisability of this practice. When, after two subsequent sessions, she still used the scores in this fashion, she was refused further access to test scores.

When professional workers outside the given agency request test data on a person, it should be cleared through channels. These channels should include a release (preferably in writing) from the examinee or his parents. Scores should not be released to nonprofessional workers outside the agency.

Industry

Within industry, certain differences in practice may be noted. The testing has usually been done at the request of the company. The company is the client, and there may be a presumption that the company can use the information as it sees fit. If there is any suggestion, however, that the company is securing information under the promise of confidence and then abusing that confidence, the company will suffer at least some loss of public respect. If test data cannot be used to the distinct advantage of the employee, it should not be revealed to anyone outside the company on any pretext—except, of course, at the request of the employee. Within industry, as elsewhere, any test data obtained as a part of therapeutic counseling (even when this has been a relationship with a psychotherapist employed full-time within the company) should never be revealed to anyone except at the request of the employee himself.

In Conversation

We do not discuss, either publicly or in casual conversation, the test results of any of our examinees. It is permissible, of course, to identify the individual and his test scores in a case conference in either a school, industrial, or clinical setting. But we cannot ethically continue our discussion of the individual outside the conference room!

COMMUNICATING THE RESULTS

The two essential steps in test interpretation are: (1) understanding the test results, and (2) communicating these results orally or in writing to another appropriate individual.

To a Trained Professional Worker

When the other person is trained in testing, the task of communicating results is relatively simple. We may start by giving the test name (including form, level, and edition—if pertinent) and the raw scores. We may include derived scores, if desired, along with the norm group(s) used. If both of us know our tests, there is every reason to believe that the information will be communicated accurately. If the information is communicated orally, we may take a few shortcuts; however, if the report is made in writing it should be complete.

When making a written report to another professional worker in whom I have confidence, I find the following method both convenient and economical:

> I include a Thermo-Fax or Verifax copy of test profiles and the like. To this, I add a short letter of transmittal pointing out any unusual aspects of the case (either about the person or his test results); I also note any irregularities in the testing procedures. If the examinee has been in counseling with me, I may include on a separate sheet a brief summary of our contacts to date, together with my observations as to probable major problem areas and my expectation of outcome. I address this material to the professional worker personally and mark it "CONFIDENTIAL."

The availability of copying machines is a tremendous boon to those who handle tests, for we can make a copy or two in several seconds at a cost of only a few cents. Furthermore, there is no danger of mistakes when making copies in this fashion.

Whenever there is the slightest doubt as to the testing knowledge of the person to whom we send test scores, we should add some further explanation of the tests and the scores.

"The *NEW Test* is a new scholastic aptitude test put out by the PDQ Company; we have been trying it out this year to see how well it compares with the *OLD Test*. The norm groups seem to be reasonably comparable, and we have found that our students tend to do about the same on both tests; however, the NEW is a little more highly speeded, and some of our teachers do not like it as well for that reason. You will note, too, that the publisher's national norms are given in stanines. I do not know whether you have been using stanines at your school, so I have included an approximate percentile value for each one. Please let me know if I can be of further help. . . ."

The aim of test interpretation is, after all, to insure that the other person understands the results of testing. We do not fulfill that purpose unless we take all reasonable steps to state the results meaningfully.

To a Professional Worker Untrained in Testing

When test data are being given to a professional worker who is relatively untrained in testing, it is advisable to give both a written report and an oral interpretation. Unquestionably some of the best work of this sort is done by school psychologists in their reports to school principals and teachers. By and large, school psychologists do a remarkably good job of working with individual children and of reporting their findings. They seem much more interested in delivering informative and helpful reports than in showing off their erudition through overuse of technical jargon.

Reports to school teachers, to members of management, to personnel workers, to academic deans, and to others who typically have limited training in testing should be drawn up very carefully. We cannot assume that they know the difference between percentage-correct scores and percentile ranks; they probably do not. We cannot assume that they know what a standard score is—or an IQ—or an age score. Our reports need to be informative, but neither subservient nor patronizing.

"Betty's PR on the *Otis* is 74," is a statement that does not mean much to a person who does not know that PR means *percentile rank,* does not know what percentile rank means, and does not know what the *Otis* is. (And this particular statement would be only a little more meaningful to those of us who do understand these points, for there are several *Otis* tests and many different norms groups.)

This form would be much more helpful:

> "On the *Blank Aptitude Test,* Betty did as well as or better than 74 per cent of the recent applicants for clerical positions with our company. We find that about ___ per cent of the girls with similar scores have maintained at least Satisfactory ratings. . . ."

Or, perhaps, this:

> "On the *Blank Aptitude Test,* Betty did as well as or better than 74 per cent of the freshmen entering our college this past September. This score suggests that she should be capable of doing the work required in her program."

To a Mature Examinee

Although much test interpretation done under this heading would come within the framework of counseling, there is some which is done independently of counseling. The trained and experienced counselor will have developed skills and techniques of his own, and the new counselor should be developing them through his specialized training and in-service supervision. We are concerned with techniques which can be used effectively and safely by relatively untrained test users.

Individuals suspected of severe maladjustment should be referred to specialists wherever possible (*see* Chapter Ten). Our examinees are presumed to be adolescents or adults who have no disabling problems.

The following list of principles is not exhaustive. Although some of these points represent my personal opinion only, I think that most of them would be accepted by nearly all experienced test users:

1. Test interpretation usually is done within some greater purposeful interview situation: e.g., counseling, guidance, placement, selection, etc. There are times, however, when the test interpretation itself is sufficient reason for the interview—especially with high school students.

2. Look over the test results before the interpretation interview. Make sure that you understand them and have some idea of what you want to say.

3. Establish a comfortable working relationship with the examinee. Be certain that you have his interest and attention.

4. Be careful of your words. Examinees can be depended upon to remember your careless remarks and to misunderstand what they do not want to hear. Your care will keep distortion to a minimum.

5. Explain something about every test variable you interpret. The examinee may know nothing about the various types of test and probably knows nothing about the specific tests he took.

6. Explain the nature of the norms groups with which he is being compared, especially when they differ for the various tests.

7. Sometimes, especially in a counseling setting, an opening like this is helpful: "How do you think you did? Do you have any idea which tests you did best on?"

8. If you feel comfortable in doing so, show the examinee the profile sheet(s); use this (them) as your basis for interpretation. Note, however, that some counselors believe that this is not a good practice and that it encourages an examinee to "read ahead" and thus pay less attention to the explanation.

9. Do not force the interpretation on the examinee. If he does not want to know the results, let him alone. You are wasting time—yours and his. Let him know that you may be available later if he changes his mind, but that you feel it is pointless to continue under these circumstances. (I can think of some exceptions, but not many; the point is that, desirable though it might be for the examinee to know his test results, he is not likely to understand them under stress.)

10. Interpret *all* of the test variables, not just those on which the examinee has done a good job. He has a right to learn his limitations as well as his strengths. (A trained counselor, though, may prefer *not* to interpret some *personality* test variables.)

11. It is more difficult to interpret low scores than high ones. Designations of high and low are somewhat arbitrary, but not entirely so. (*See* the suggestions at the end of this chapter.)

12. Low scores are more easily accepted if they are stated in objective terms, such as: "Of people with scores like yours, only 10 per cent have managed to maintain a passing average and to graduate in that curriculum." (*See* Expectancy Tables, pages 66-71.)

13. Sometimes low scores may be made easier to accept when the nature of the test is slightly distorted. I sometimes point out to a student who has done poorly on an intelligence or scholastic aptitude test: "This means that you are very low in book-learning ability when compared with other high school juniors nationally. A few students with scores like yours may succeed in college through very efficient planning and extra-hard studying, but your high school grades suggest that you do not achieve well in the actual class situation."

14. Sometimes low scores can be gotten across through an analogous statement: "A college director of admissions is like anyone else. He likes to bet on the winners. He knows that students with better high school grades and higher test scores than yours are more likely to do well in college. Like a gambler, he will sometimes play a long shot and will be delighted when one pays off. But, for the most part, he has to select those people who seem most likely to succeed."

15. Never make a direct prediction, such as: "This score means that you will never make it to college," or "This test score proves that you would never succeed on this job," or "With scores like these, you are a cinch to get through college with flying colors." You can be very, very wrong! You are much safer to talk in group terms, such as: "Very few students with such scores . . ." or "Most students with scores such as these are able to do well in college if they study reasonably hard."

16. Do not assume that your examinee will remember everything. Try to help him to remember the important elements by summarizing the results; perhaps something like this: "In general, then, you show average or better ability to learn, and you show near-average achievement in most areas. But you seem to be lower than we would expect in dealing with abstract or mathematical reasoning."

17. If appropriate, make general suggestions: "Our company will not promote men who have low scores on tests of verbal ability. Have you considered going to night school? You could pick up an English course or two that might be helpful—and our company policy is to pay at least part of the expense." Or, perhaps: "Your scores suggest that you may have difficulty in getting into medical school. On the other hand, you do have good grades here in high school— and this is important. You might be wise to select a small liberal arts college where you can hope for more individual attention and

try for good grades in premedical work. Perhaps you will make it. Just to be on the safe side, though, you may want to consider some possible alternatives if you do not make med school. Sometimes people find it very difficult if they have given no thought to other things and then have to change plans at the last minute." Or, perhaps: "You have scored very high in the various English tests. Have you ever thought of working on the school paper? You might find it very rewarding."

18. Do not forget: the examinee decides what he will do. As a test interpreter, you may make suggestions but not decisions. (As an academic dean, placement director, etc. you may make institutional decisions; the examinee makes individual decisions.)

19. Test interpretation often provides a good way of opening a discussion of the examinee's problems, plans for the future, etc. If you are not a trained counselor, decide in advance how far you can go in receiving the examinee's confidences.

20. Never interpret an examinee's scores solely in writing. Supplementary interpretation, especially through interpretive folders such as those mentioned in Chapter Seven, may be very helpful. Most counselors feel strongly, however, that we should not rely exclusively on written interpretations because they offer no opportunity for counselee "feedback."

21. Most important of all: know what you are doing, and do what seems natural and effective.

To a Child

Some teachers try to explain achievement test results to elementary school children, especially when using the results in deciding in what areas the pupils may need to give special attention. Other than this, little effort is made to interpret tests to children who are below high school age.

I think that this is unfortunate. Children have considerable capacity for understanding and have tremendous curiosity. Many will disagree, but I believe that some basic interpretation could be done effectively with children as young as ten years of age. The teacher might discuss the general nature of the tests with the class as a group. This could be followed up by an individual conference with each of the pupils, perhaps focusing attention mainly on areas of highest and lowest achievement and a statement about his achievement relative to his ability (without saying much about his intelligence itself). Such interpretations would need to be handled carefully, but could help youngsters in their search for an understanding of themselves.

Even with children of junior and senior high school age, most test interpretation should be couched in general terms. Children like to see things in black-and-white terms and are likely to oversimplify or overgeneralize. They are not likely to remember the test limitations as well as they remember specific facts which are mentioned casually or incidentally.

Superior students can handle somewhat more detailed interpretations. The interpretation can perhaps be used as an opportunity for emphasizing the importance of acquiring good study habits and developing a sound background for future work.

Special care must be used when interpreting results to children of below-average ability in order not to discourage them from trying to do their best. In dealing with this problem, the skilled counselor should be able to help the older child come to an acceptance of his limitations and to an appreciation of what can reasonably be accomplished through sustained effort. There is little kindness in encouraging unrealistic ambitions in the below-average child, but it is cruel to make the child feel that he is worthless and stupid.

> One of my graduate students recently reported the following incident to me. Her son, Tommy, came home and said that he had gotten an A on a standardized achievement test battery. Tommy's second-grade teacher, it developed, had announced aloud in class letter-grade equivalents (including F's) for the test performance of every pupil. Such letter grades exist only in the teacher's mind— they are not given in the manual!
>
> This incident, of course, is an example of bad interpretation. No second-grader is likely to learn much from such a procedure, and with few exceptions (e.g., a scholarship competition) public announcement of test scores is grossly unethical.

To Parents

Very much the same considerations are involved in interpreting test scores to parents as are involved when interpreting scores to mature examinees. Parents, though, are more likely to be argumentative and to question the accuracy of the test results. Parents of dull children are likely to be very sensitive, and special caution must be used to make the parents view the results as objectively as possible. They must not be allowed to develop hostility toward the child because "he's so dumb," nor should they be given encouragement (probably false unless the child is only slightly retarded) that he's "just passing through a phase."

Parents of a child of superior intellect may question why he is not doing better work and getting better grades if he is so intelligent. They may also question whether the school is doing its part in challenging the child to do his best work. (Consider carefully whether some such criticism may not be justified. Is the school doing what it can to meet the needs of the superior youngster?)

Parents differ markedly in their ability to understand and accept test results. I would have no hesitancy in discussing actual scores (IQ's, percentile ranks, or whatever) with some mature parents. With others, defensive from the start, I shudder at the thought of giving any sort of interpretation. Be careful! And try to know beforehand how detailed an interpretation you will give.

High and Low

How is high is high? Your answer is probably as good as anyone else's. Except for a few considerations, it is a completely arbitrary decision.

First, we need to remember that scores are never completely accurate. Therefore, we should never say that any score is high unless it is at least one or two standard errors of measurement above the mean; otherwise, the above-average score probably differs from the mean only by chance. The same line of reasoning, of course, operates in calling scores low.

Second, we must remember the way in which scores tend to cluster about the mean in typical distributions of test scores. The distance between successive percentile values is very small near the middle of the distribution. Thus a change in percentile ranks reflects only a slight change in raw scores near the average, but a large change in raw scores near the extremes.

Third, we have to remember that scores used in reporting standardized tests are relative rather than absolute. A given raw score may place an examinee high when compared with one group, but low when compared with another group.

Fourth, because of the greater reliability (and relatively smaller standard errors of measurement) of some tests, we may have more confidence in our use of high and low with these tests than with other, less reliable, tests.

I generally use the following descriptive scale:

Percentile Ranks	Descriptive Terms
95 or above	Very high; superior
85-95	High; excellent
75-85	Above average; good
25-75	About average; satisfactory or fair
15-25	Below average; fair or slightly weak
5-15	Low; weak
5 or below	Very low; very weak

This is not an inflexible standard, but I think that it is a helpful one. Sometimes we vary these designations, or apply more (or less) rigorous standards.

If a graduate engineer were being compared on company norms with general clerical employees (perhaps the only norms the company has for the test), we might regard a percentile rank of 88 as being only "satisfactory" or "reasonably good."

In the same way, a graduate student who scores near the eightieth percentile on national undergraduate norms is probably only "about average."

Chapter Ten # EXPERTS STILL NEEDED

We have touched on some of the most important topics in psychological and educational testing, but there is a great deal that we have not mentioned. One important consideration is the persistent demand for experts in measurement.

For example, we have barely mentioned tests of typical performance. Such tests have their proper place in the hands of thoroughly trained counseling or clinical psychologists. When properly used by qualified persons, typical performance tests may give clues to the personality dynamics of both normal and disturbed people. Their interpretation demands skills and knowledge beyond those covered in this book (although a reasonable job of interpreting interest tests and some simple inventory-style personality tests should not be much beyond the competence of the reader).

Projective tests, certainly, should be interpreted only by well-trained psychologists. And the diversity of projective techniques is so great that some degree of training is needed in each of the specific techniques that the psychologist uses. Projective techniques are not parlor games or classroom exercises for the personal amusement of the test user.

Even with tests of maximum performance, there are some areas which are best left to the expert. Individual tests of intelligence, for example, require special training of the examiner. The trained examiner should be the one, too, to report the results of individual intelligence tests, for the report should include much more than a mere test score; otherwise, the situation does not require the use of an individual test in the first place.

Throughout this book (and especially in Chapter Nine), we have considered briefly some implications of testing for guidance and counseling. On the other hand, we have recognized that the most effective use of tests in guidance and counseling situations requires much more knowledge than can be acquired from this book. There is a need for professional counselors and guidance workers—people who can get the fullest meaning out of test results and employ this meaning in their interviews.

Experts in tests and measurements are needed, too, to construct and validate new tests, to conduct research with tests, to advance measurement theory, etc.

There should be at least one top-flight test specialist within each school system, each college, and each large industrial corporation. This specialist and his staff should have such varied duties as the following:

1. Keeping up-to-date on theoretical measurement; there is some excellent work being done that has not yet trickled down to the test user.
2. Maintaining a file of tests, both old and new, which might be consulted by other professional workers; this file would include manuals and catalogs.
3. Maintaining a library of books and periodical publications on tests and measurements.
4. Directing any major research activity involving tests.
5. Serving as adviser or consultant to people in the organization who want to do their own test-related research.
6. Evaluating new tests for possible use within the organization.
7. Selecting new tests for use within the organization.
8. Preparing local norms for tests.
9. Discussing test-related problems, issues, and questions with interested personnel both within and outside the organization.
10. Conducting in-service training programs for all people in the organization who work with tests.

The need for such specialists is obvious. So many tests are available that experts are needed to evaluate them and to select those which best meet the demands of their local situation. Then, too, there must be someone who can serve as a resource person for all those who use tests within an organization.

Chapter Eleven

CONCLUDING REMARKS

Are there some general principles which summarize the message of this book? Probably, and since this is likely to be the most widely read chapter, I shall try to list here some of the most important ones.

Know the Test

There is no substitute for knowledge of the test that is being interpreted. Test titles are not always descriptive of the actual test content; furthermore, many terms can be defined differently by different people. The underlying rationale of a test may be very important to our understanding of it. Our interpretation of test results may differ for power and speeded tests, for individual and group tests, etc. We should read the test manual of any test we plan to interpret. Whenever practicable, test selection should be made only by people with sufficient background in measurement to understand the technical data descriptive of the test.

Know the Norms

It is especially important for us to know what norms are being used. We cannot interpret adequately without understanding what group our test scores are being compared with. We may want to use several different norm groups when they are available. For example, we may want to compare a high school senior's scores with both high school seniors and college freshmen, or a person's aptitude test results with both applicants and with present employees, etc. In many situations, we may want to develop our own local norms.

Know the Score

It is always good to "know the score" in the slang sense of that term; however, here we are being literal. We need to know whether a given number is a standard score (and what kind), a percentile rank, a raw score, or something else. Fantastic misunderstandings can result from confusing different types of score. We have used a new classification scheme in explaining test scores (*see* Chapter Six).

Know the Background

Test results do not tell the entire story, and we should not expect them to. We must consider all available information—whether or not it comes from a test.

Communicate Effectively

In many settings, we will have to communicate test results to others. To get the interpretation across to an examinee, we must be certain to give the examinee all pertinent information. For example, we should give him some indication of what the norm group is like, how he compares with that group, and what the test is supposed to measure. This, of course, is not sufficient; after all, the examinee may very well resist accepting any interpretation that differs from his own conception of himself. Several techniques that I have found helpful are mentioned in Chapter Nine.

Use the Test

Not too surprisingly, we can come to a better understanding of what a test is like by using it. As we develop more experience in working with tests, we can attempt some simple studies to see how well a particular test works out for our own specific purposes. As we develop competence along research lines, we can have increased confidence in the interpretations.

Use Caution

Test scores *reflect* ability; they *do not determine* ability. Test scores may *suggest*, but never *prove*. We are much safer when we make interpretations based on the actual performance of those who have had similar scores (*see* Expectancy Tables on pages 66-71) than when we try to tell an examinee, "This score means that *you* will . . ."

Consult the Expert

Testing can get very technical, and there are many subtleties not even hinted at in this book. There is still need for a testing specialist wherever tests are widely used. And this specialist should be freely available to those who would like his assistance.

Go Ahead and Try!

There are many pitfalls to the use of tests and their proper interpretation. There are all sorts of limitations to tests and to test scores. But tests *can* be helpful. Do not be overly cautious or you will never get any testing done. Go ahead and try!

BIBLIOGRAPHY

General References

1. Buros, Oscar K. (ed.). *The Fifth Mental Measurements Yearbook.* Highland Park, N. J.: Gryphon Press, 1959. (This volume and the four which precede it are essential references for those interested in critical reviews of tests.)
2. Cottle, William C. & N. M. Downie. *Procedures and Preparation for Counseling.* Englewood Cliffs, N. J.: Prentice-Hall, Inc., 1960. (Some very good chapters on testing.)
3. Cronbach, Lee J. & Goldine Gleser. *Psychological Tests and Personnel Decisions.* Urbana: University of Illinois Press, 1957. (Book stresses role of tests in making of individual and institutional decisions; highly technical.)
4. Durost, Walter N. & George A. Prescott. *Essentials of Measurement for Teachers.* New York: Harcourt, Brace & World, Inc., 1962. (Over-ambitious title, but much excellent material—especially on use of stanines.)
5. *Ethical Standards of Psychologists.* Washington: American Psychological Association, 1953. (Some sections on ethics of test usage.)
6. Flanagan, John C. *et al. The Talents of American Youth: 1. Design for a Study of American Youth.* Boston: Houghton Mifflin Company, 1962. (Includes a description of the varied tests used in Project TALENT.)
7. Goldman, Leo. *Using Tests in Counseling.* New York: Appleton-Century-Crofts, Inc., 1962. (Some excellent material in a scholarly book.)
8. Gulliksen, Harold. *Theory of Mental Tests.* New York: John Wiley & Sons, Inc., 1950. (The classic in test theory; extremely difficult, but rewarding reading.)
9. Lindquist, E. F. (ed.). *Educational Measurement.* Washington:

American Council on Education, 1951. (Encyclopedic and uneven in coverage and difficulty, but a superb reference.)

10. Seashore, Harold (ed.). *Test Service Notebooks.* New York: The Psychological Corporation. (An excellent series of gratis publications, each on some aspect of testing. Write them—they'll be glad to put you on their mailing list.)

11. Super, Donald E. & John O. Crites. *Appraisal of Vocational Fitness by Means of Psychological Tests* (rev. ed.). New York: Harper and Row, 1962. (A long book and occasionally difficult to read, but just about the best source of information on test interpretation.)

12. *Technical Recommendations for Achievement Tests.* Washington: National Education Association, 1955. (Excellent material for study of test evaluation; *see also* next reference.)

13. "Technical Recommendations for Psychological Tests and Diagnostic Techniques." *Psychological Bulletin,* 1954, v. **51** supplement. (Excellent, interesting, and informative; *see also* Reference 12, above.)

14. Thorndike, Robert L. *Personnel Selection.* New York: John Wiley & Sons, Inc., 1949. (Primarily industrial applications; excellent, but dated.)

15. Travers, Robert M. W. *How to Make Achievement Tests.* New York: The Odyssey Press, Inc., 1950. (Especially helpful on item-writing.)

16. Traxler, Arthur E. *Techniques of Guidance* (rev. ed.). New York: Harper and Row, 1957. (Good source for guidance forms and the like; much practical information about testing.)

17. Wood, Dorothy Adkins. *Test Construction.* Columbus, Ohio: Charles E. Merrill Books, Inc., 1960. (A thorough, but concise and readable job—as only this author could do it!)

Selected Measurements Textbooks

[As a general rule, those which are *primarily educational* tend to be easier to read, but perhaps less thorough—except on achievement tests; those which are *primarily psychological* usually include more material on test statistics and personality tests, and give a wider variety of examples. I have used (and like) the books by: Anastasi, Cronbach, Ross & Stanley, and Thorndike & Hagen; however, I believe that the others have merit, too.]

Primarily Psychological

1. Anastasi, Anne. *Psychological Testing* (2d ed.). New York: The Macmillan Co., 1961.

2. Cronbach, Lee J. *Essentials of Psychological Testing* (2d ed.). New York: Harper and Row, 1960.

3. Freeman, Frank S. *Theory and Practice of Psychological Testing.* New York: Holt, Rinehart & Winston, Inc., 1950.
4. Greene, Edward B. *Measurements of Human Behavior* (rev. ed.). New York: The Odyssey Press, Inc., 1952.

Primarily Educational

1. Ahmann, J. Stanley & Marvin D. Glock. *Evaluating Pupil Growth.* Boston: Allyn and Bacon, Inc., 1959.
2. Baron, Denis & Harold W. Bernard. *Evaluation Techniques for Classroom Teachers.* New York: McGraw-Hill Book Co., Inc., 1958.
3. Darley, John G. *Testing and Counseling in the High-School Guidance Program.* Chicago: Science Research Associates, 1943.
4. Jordan, A. M. *Measurement in Education.* New York: McGraw-Hill Book Co., Inc., 1953.
5. Noll, Victor. *Introduction to Educational Measurement.* Boston: Houghton Mifflin Company, 1957.
6. Nunnally, Jum C., Jr. *Tests and Measurements.* New York: McGraw-Hill Book Co., Inc., 1959.
7. Remmers, H. H. *Practical Introduction to Measurement and Evaluation.* New York: Harper and Row, 1960.
8. Ross, C. C. & Julian Stanley. *Measurement in Today's Schools* (3d ed.). Englewood Cliffs, N. J.: Prentice-Hall, Inc., 1954.
9. Thorndike, Robert L. & Elizabeth Hagen. *Measurement and Evaluation in Psychology and Education* (2d ed.). New York: John Wiley & Sons, Inc., 1961.
10. Travers, Robert M. W. *Educational Measurement.* New York: The Macmillan Co., 1955.
11. Traxler, Arthur *et al. Introduction to Testing and the Use of Test Results in Public Schools.* New York: Harper and Row, 1953.

Films

A series of five films, each about 15 minutes in length, has been produced by the *Cooperative Test Division, Educational Testing Service, Princeton, N. J.* Each film centers on a single problem: e.g., selecting achievement tests, interpreting test scores, using test results, etc. They are excellent for showing to measurements classes, teacher groups, PTA meetings, and the like. They may be borrowed or purchased from ETS. For further information, write them at the address above.

APPENDIX

GLOSSARY
OF TERMS

This Glossary of Terms, like the rest of the book, is intended primarily for those who have had little formal training in testing. Therefore, some of the definitions may not meet the more exacting requirements of professional measurements people. Because most of the terms are discussed elsewhere in the book, I have tried to keep these definitions brief. The designation of various derived scores according to Types refers to the classification scheme presented in Chapter Six.

Although most definitions in this Glossary come from my personal notes, I did make occasional reference to recent Glossaries prepared by the California Test Bureau and by the World Book Company (now, Harcourt, Brace & World, Inc.), and to three professional dictionaries:

1. *A Glossary of Measurement Terms*, California Test Bureau, Los Angeles, n.d.
2. English, Horace B. and Ava Champney English, *A Comprehensive Dictionary of Psychological and Psychoanalytical Terms*. New York: Longmans, Green and Co., 1958.
3. Good, Carter V., ed., *Dictionary of Education* (2nd ed.). New York: McGraw-Hill Book Company, Inc., 1959.
4. Kendall, Maurice G. and William R. Buckland, *A Dictionary of Statistical Terms*. Edinburgh: Oliver and Boyd, 1957. (Issued in the United States by Hafner Publishing Co., New York.)

5. Lennon, Roger T., "A Glossary of 100 Measurement Terms," *Test Service Notebook*, No. 13. Tarrytown-on-Hudson: Harcourt, Brace & World, Inc., n.d.

References 1 and 5 are available gratis from their respective publishers. Both are convenient, well-prepared lists covering about the same terms defined here; however, their definitions may be somewhat more comprehensive on selected terms.

References 2 and 3 are technical dictionaries which should be helpful and intelligible to the readers of this book. My definitions may resemble some of those in Good's *Dictionary of Education*, for I was a contributor to that volume. The English and English volume is especially helpful in showing differences in shade of meaning; besides, the late Dr. English's style of presentation is delightful!

Reference 4, Kendall and Buckland, is highly technical. Its definitions are likely to be more intelligible to the professional statistician than to the beginner.

accomplishment quotient (AQ). A derived score (Type III D) which is equal to the ratio between *educational age* and *mental age* (EA/MA); sometimes called "achievement quotient."

achievement age. See *educational age.*

achievement battery. A *battery* of *achievement tests.*

achievement test. A test designed to measure the amount of knowledge and/or skill a person has acquired, usually as a result of classroom instruction; may be either *informal* or *standardized.*

adjustment inventory. See *personality test.*

age equivalent. The chronological age for which a specified raw score is the average raw score.

age norms. *Norms* which give *age equivalents* for raw-score values.

age score. See *age equivalent.*

alternate-form reliability. A method of estimating test *reliability* by the *correlation coefficient* between two equivalent or parallel forms of the test; based on consistency of content.

anticipated-achievement grade-placement score. A concept used by the California Test Bureau to indicate the average grade-placement score made on an achievement test by pupils having a specified mental age and grade placement.

aptitude. That combination of characteristics, both native and acquired, which indicate the capacity of a person to develop proficiency in some skill or subject matter after relevant training; usually, but not necessarily, implies intellectual or skill aspects rather than emotional or personality characteristics.

arithmetic mean. See *mean.*

articulation. Act or process of developing different *editions, forms,* and (especially) *levels* of the same test to yield results that are comparable.

average. A general term for any central tendency measure; most commonly used in testing are the *mean, median,* and *mode.*

battery. (1) A set of tests standardized on the same group, so that the results will be comparable; such a battery is called "integrated." (2) A set of tests administered at about the same time to an individual or group; e.g., an employment battery, counseling battery, or admissions battery.

C-score. A *normalized standard score* (Type II B 4 c) of eleven units.

chronological age (CA). Any person's age; i.e., the length of time he has lived. The CA is used in determining *intelligence quotients* and is a factor to consider when interpreting certain types of scores, especially age scores.

class interval. The unit of a *frequency distribution,* especially when the unit is greater than one; a band of score values assumed to be equal for purposes of computation or graphing.

coefficient of correlation. An index number indicating the degree of relationship between two variables, i.e., the tendency for values of one variable to change systematically with changes in values of a second variable; no relationship $= 0.00$, a perfect relationship $= \pm 1.00$. [Although there are different coefficients for various purposes, the basic type is the Pearson product-moment correlation (r) which is used when both variables are *continuous,* distributed symmetrically, etc.]

concurrent validity. *Empirical validity* when both test scores and *criterion* values are obtained at about the same time.

construct validity. Test validation based on a combination of logical and empirical evidence of the relationship between the test and a related theory; concerned with the psychological meaningfulness of the test.

content reliability. The consistency with which a test measures whatever it measures; may be estimated by a *reliability coefficient* based on: (a) *split halves,* (b) *alternate forms,* or (c) *internal consistency.*

content validity. Logical evidence that the item content of a test is suitable for the purpose for which the test is to be used; concept is used principally with achievement tests.

continuous variable. A *variable* capable, actually or theoretically, of assuming any value—as opposed to a *discrete variable,* which may take only whole-number values; test scores are treated as being continuous although they are less obvious examples than time, distance, weight, etc.

correction-for-guessing formula. A formula sometimes used in scoring objective tests to make an allowance for items that have been "guessed" correctly; general formula is: $X_c = R - (W/A - 1)$, where $X_c =$ corrected score, $R =$ number of items right, $W =$ number of items wrong, and $A =$ number of alternative choices per item. Although the underlying reasoning is dubious, the formula has considerable merit when examinees differ greatly in number of items left unanswered; use of the formula does not change order of scores when no one omits any items.

correlation. Tendency for two (or occasionally more) variables to change values concomitantly. Note: evidence of correlation is not evidence of causation. See *coefficient of correlation.*

criterion. A standard against which a test may be validated; e.g., grade-pòint average is an obvious criterion for a scholastic aptitude test.

criterion-keying. The act or process of developing a test's scoring key empirically, through noting characteristic differences in answers made by different groups of individuals.

cross-validation. The act or process of verifying results obtained on one group (or one study) by replication with a different, but similar, group (or study).

curriculum validity. See *content validity.*

decile. Any one of the nine percentile points which divide a distribution into ten subgroups of equal frequency; e.g., the first decile (D_1) is the same as the tenth percentile (P_{10}).

decile rank. A derived score (Type II B 5) expressed in terms of the nearest *decile;* thus, a decile rank of 1 is given to any value between the fifth and fifteenth percentiles. Note: a decile rank of 0 is given to values below the fifth percentile; a decile rank of 10 to any value above the ninety-fifth percentile.

derived score. Any type of score other than a raw score.

deviation. The amount by which a score differs from a specified reference point (usually, but not always, the mean or other average).

deviation IQ. (1) A standard score (Type II A 5·) with a mean fixed statistically at 100 and standard deviation fixed according to the wish of the test's author; has advantages over the *ratio IQ*, which it is designed to approximate. (2) A normalized standard score (Type II B 4 e) designed to resemble a *ratio IQ*, but possessing certain advantages. (3) A derived score (Type IV C) in which IQ is equal to 100 plus the amount by which an examinee's raw score deviates from the *norm* for his age.

diagnostic test. (1) A test (usually of achievement) designed to diagnose specific educational and study difficulties. (2) Any test given in connection with counseling or psychotherapy as an aid to diagnosing an individual's mental disorder, possible maladjustment, etc.

difficulty value. A statement of a test item's difficulty, usually expressed as the percentage of individuals in a given group answering the item correctly.

discrete value. A value obtained through counting rather than measuring; thus, can take only whole-number values—e.g., number of employees in each plant, number of books in school libraries, number of students in each classroom, etc.; unlike *continuous* variables which can assume any value.

discrimination value. Any of several statistics used to express the extent to which a test item shows a difference between high-ability and low-ability examinees.

distracter. Any incorrect alternative in a multiple-choice item.

distribution. See *frequency distribution; normal distribution.*

educational age. A derived score (Type II D 1 b) in which the examinee's performance on an achievement test is stated as the age for which his performance is average; analogous to *mental age* scores on an intelligence test.

empirical validity. Test validity based on data from actual studies; e.g., as evidenced by coefficient of correlation between test scores and criterion values.

equivalent form. Any of two or more forms (or versions) of a test, usually (but not always) standardized on the same population and published at the same time—which forms are designed to be similar in item content and difficulty, so that scores on the forms will be similar.

error. A generic term for those elements in a test and testing situation which operate to keep a test from giving perfectly valid results: (a) *constant errors* have a direct adverse effect on validity, but may not affect reliability (e.g., having arithmetic items in an English test); (b) *variable* (or *random*) *errors* reduce reliability directly and validity indirectly (e.g., nonstandard conditions of test administration, chance passing or failing of items, ambiguous wording of test items, etc.). Note: errors are inherent in all measurement, but mistakes are not; we can estimate the amount of *variable error* present, but not the amount (or the presence) of mistakes.

essay test. See *subjective test.*

expectancy table. Any table showing class intervals of test scores (or other predictor variable) along one axis, and criterion categories (or similar information) along the other axis; entries show number or, more typically, percentage of individuals within specified score intervals who have achieved at a given level on the criterion variable.

extrapolation. The act or process of estimating values beyond those actually obtained; e.g., extreme values for both age and grade-placement scores have to be established in this manner.

face validity. Superficial appearance of validity; i.e., test looks as if it should measure what is intended (regardless of the presence or absence of data indicating that it is actually valid for some purpose).

factor. (1) Strictly and technically, an element or variable presumed to exist because of its ability to help explain some of the interrelationships noted among a set of tests. (2) Equally properly, the ability or characteristic represented by a *factor* (def. 1, above). (3) Loosely, anything which is partially responsible for a result or outcome (e.g., "study is an important factor in obtaining good grades").

factor analysis. Any of several complex statistical procedures for analyzing the intercorrelations among a set of tests (or other variables) for the purpose of identifying those *factors* (defs. 1 and 2), preferably few in number, which cause the intercorrelations; widely used in efforts to understand the organization of intelligence, personality, and the like.

frequency. The number of individuals obtaining any specified score or falling in any specified class interval.

frequency distribution. Any orderly arrangement of scores, usually from highest to lowest, showing the number of individuals (i.e., the frequency) making each score or falling in each class interval.

frequency polygon. A type of graph used commonly to portray a distribution of test scores (or values of some other continuous variable).

grade equivalent. See *grade-placement score.*

grade norm. The average test score obtained by pupils with a specified grade placement.

grade-placement score. A derived score (Type II D 2) which is expressed as the grade placement of those pupils for whom a given score was average; e.g., a grade-placement score of 7.3 indicates average performance for pupils in the third month of the seventh grade.

group test. A test designed to be administered simultaneously to a group of examinees by one examiner.

individual decision. A term used by Cronbach and Gleser to describe the situation in which a choice must be made by the individual (or, sometimes, on his behalf) rather than by an institution; e.g., the choice of a career.

individual test. A test which usually, if not always, can be administered to only one examinee at a time.

informal test. Any test intended primarily for the use of the test constructor; used in opposition to *standardized test.*

institutional decision. A term used by Cronbach and Gleser to describe the situation in which a choice must be made on behalf of an institution (a school or company) rather than by the individuals tested; e.g., which applicants to select and which to reject. Tests are demonstrably superior in such situations than in situations demanding *individual decisions.*

intellectual status index. A derived score (Type III B) used by the California Test Bureau; similar to a *ratio IQ* except that, instead of the child's actual chronological age being used, the average chronological age of pupils with his same grade placement is substituted.

intelligence. An abstraction variously defined by various authorities; in general, that capacity or set of capacities which enable an individual to learn, to cope with his environment, to solve problems, etc.

intelligence quotient (IQ). See *deviation IQ; ratio IQ.*

internal consistency. A term referring to any of several techniques for estimating the *content reliability* of a test through knowledge of *item analysis* statistics.

interpolation. The act or process of estimating a value which falls between two known or computed values; this practice is often followed in establishing age and grade-placement scores, so that the norms table will cover all possible ages or grade-placements (e.g., samples of children aged 7-0 and 7-3 may have been tested and their average scores established as being 7-0 and 7-3, respectively; intermediate scores would be assigned values of 7-1 and 7-2 by interpolation).

inventory. (1) Most commonly used to describe a *paper-and-pencil* test of personality, interest, attitude, or the like. (2) Less commonly used to describe an achievement test designed to "take an inventory" of student or class knowledge or skill on a specific task.

item. (1) Any individual problem or question on a test. (2) Usually, but not always, the basic scorable unit of an *objective* test.

item analysis. The act or process of examining a test item empirically to determine: (a) its *difficulty value,* and (b) its *discrimination value.* Note: such values will differ somewhat from group to group and from time to time.

key, scoring. (1) The collection of correct answers (or scored responses) for the items of a test. (2) The device or sheet, containing the scored responses, which is used in scoring the test.

Kuder-Richardson formula. Any of several formulas developed by Kuder and Richardson for the estimation of *content reliability* through an *internal-consistency* analysis.

machine-scoring. The act or process of scoring a test with the aid of a mechanical or electrical device which counts and may record the scored responses of a test (or subtest); the most common machines involve one or more of these processes: (a) *mark-sensing,* (b) *punched-hole,* or (c) electronic scanning.

mark-sensing. Descriptive of a system of *machine-scoring* tests which uses an electrical contact to "sense" responses to be scored.

maximum-performance test.   Any test on which the examinee is directed, at least implicitly, to do the best job he can; e.g., intelligence, aptitude, and achievement tests. Used in opposition to *typical-performance test.*

mean.   Most widely used measure of central tendency; equals the sum of scores divided by the number of examinees.

median.   Next to the mean, the most common measure of central tendency; the point on the scale of score values which separates the group into two equal subgroups; the fiftieth percentile (P_{50}), second quartile (Q_2), and the fifth decile (D_5).

mental age.   A derived score (Type II D 1 a), used on intelligence tests only, which is expressed as the age for which a given raw score is average or typical; e.g., a mental age of 12-4 indicates intelligence test performance that is average for children of twelve years four months of age.

modal age.   The chronological age that is most typical of children with a given grade placement in school.

modal-age norms.   Norms based only on those pupils near the modal age for their actual grade placement; such norms are used on most school-level achievement batteries as a presumed refinement in establishing *grade-placement scores.*

mode.   A measure of central tendency; that score value which has the highest *frequency;* i.e., that score obtained by more examinees than any other.

N.   Symbol used in this book to represent number of examinees in any specified group.

norm.   Average, normal, or standard for a group of specified status (e.g., of a given age or grade placement).

normal distribution (curve).   A useful mathematical model which represents the distribution expected when an infinite number of observations (e.g., scores) deviate from the mean only by chance; although a normal distribution can never be attained in reality, many actual distributions do approach this model. The curve drawn to portray the normal distribution is a symmetrical bell-shaped curve whose properties are completely known.

normalized standard score.   Any of several scores (Type II B) which resemble standard scores (Type II A), but which make the obtained distribution conform more closely to a normal distribution through the use of percentile equivalents.

norms.   A set of values descriptive of the performance on a test of some specified group; usually shown as a table giving equivalent values of some *derived score* for each raw score on the test.

objective test.   A test for which the scoring procedure is specified completely in advance, thereby permitting complete agreement among different scorers.

omnibus test. A test, usually of intelligence, in which items of many different types are used in obtaining a single over-all total score; usually has one set of directions and one over-all time limit.

paper-and-pencil test. Any test which requires no materials other than paper, pencil, and test booklet; most group tests are paper-and-pencil tests.

parameter. A summary or descriptive value (e.g., mean or standard deviation) for a *population* or universe; i.e., a parameter is to a *population* as a statistic is to a *sample.*

percentage-correct score. A derived score (Type I A) which expresses the examinee's performance as a percentage of the maximum possible score; frequently overlooked is the fact that such scores are more a function of item difficulty than a true measure of an examinee's absolute performance.

percentile (P). Any of the ninety-nine points along the scale of score values which divide a distribution into one hundred groups of equal frequency; e.g., P_{73} is that point below which fall 73 per cent of the cases in a distribution.

percentile rank (PR). A derived score (Type II B 2) stated in terms of the percentage of examinees in a specified group who fall below a given score point.

performance test. An ambiguous term used variously to mean: (a) a test involving special apparatus, as opposed to a *paper-and-pencil* test; (b) a test minimizing verbal skills; or (c) a work-sample test. All of these uses are unfortunate, because the term "performance" already means "the behavior of an examinee on a given test," "the score of any specified examinee on a test," etc.

personality test. A *typical-performance* test, questionnaire, or other device designed to measure some affective characteristic of the individual.

population. Any entire group so designated; i.e., the total group which is of interest or concern. As commonly used in testing, refers to the totality about which statistical inferences are to be made and from which a *sample* is taken.

power test. Any *maximum-performance* test for which speed is not an important determinant of score; thus, a test with no time limit or with a very generous time limit.

predictive validity. *Empirical validity* where criterion values are obtained subsequent to the determination of the test scores.

probable error (PE). A measure of variability, rarely used today, found by multiplying 0.6745 by either the *standard deviation* (to obtain the probable error of a distribution) or the *standard error* (to obtain the probable error of some statistic). In a normal distribution, one-half the cases lie within ± 1 PE of the mean.

profile.   A graphic representation of the performance of an individual (or, less commonly, a group) on a series of tests, especially the tests in an integrated *battery.*

prognostic test.   A test used to predict future performance (usually, success or failure) in a particular task.

projective technique.   Any method of personality measurement or study which makes use of deliberately ambiguous stimuli (e.g., ink blots, incomplete sentences, etc.) into which the examinee must "project" his personality when responding.

punched-hole.   Descriptive of a system of *machine-scoring* tests; utilizes holes punched into cards (e.g., IBM cards).

quartile.   Any of the three points which divide a frequency distribution into four groups of equal frequency. The first quartile (Q_1) equals the twenty-fifth percentile (P_{25}); $Q_2 = P_{50} = $ median; and $Q_3 = P_{75}$.

r.   Symbol for Pearson product-moment *correlation coefficient.*

random error.   See *variable error.*

random sample.   A sample drawn from a *population* in such a manner that each member has an equal chance of being selected; samples so drawn are unbiased and should yield statistics "representative" of the population.

range.   The difference between highest and lowest scores made on a test by a specified group.

ratio IQ.   A derived score (Type III A), being used less and less commonly, found by the formula: 100 (MA/CA), where MA = mental age determined from a test, and CA = chronological age (an adjusted chronological age being used for older adolescents and for adults).

raw score.   The basic score initially obtained from scoring a test according to directions given by the test maker; usually equal to number of correct responses, but may be number of wrong answers or errors, time required for a task, etc.

reliability.   Consistency or stability of a test or other measuring instrument; necessary for, but not sufficient for, *validity.* Commonly expressed as a *reliability coefficient* or a *standard error of measurement.*

reliability coefficient.   A *coefficient of correlation* designed to estimate a test's *reliability* by correlating: (a) scores on equivalent forms, (b) scores on matched halves (corrected for length), or (c) scores on two administrations of same test. May be a correlation estimate based on *internal consistency.*

sample.   A general term referring to a group, however selected, assumed to represent an entire *population.*

scaled score.   (1) Loosely, any derived score. (2) More technically, any of several systems of scores (usually similar to *standard scores*) used in: (a) articulating different forms, editions, and/or levels of a test; or (b) developmental research.

scorer reliability. Evidence that the same test responses will be similarly scored by different scorers or by the same scorer at different times.

sigma. Greek letter widely used in statistics. Capital sigma (Σ) means "to add" or "find the sum of." Lower case sigma (σ) is often used to mean *standard deviation,* especially of a *population;* however, *s* has been used in this book, rather than σ.

skewed (distribution). A noticeably asymmetrical distribution of scores. A distribution with many high scores and very few low scores is said to be "skewed to the left" or "negatively skewed."

Spearman-Brown (prophecy) formula. A formula designed to estimate the reliability that a test will have if its length is changed and other factors remain constant; most commonly used in "correcting" *split-half reliability coefficients.*

speed test. (1) A test on which an examinee's speed is an important determinant of his score. (2) A test on which the score equals the time taken to complete it.

split-half reliability coefficient. An estimate of content reliability based on the correlation between scores on two halves of a test; usually, the odd and even items are scored separately to provide these two half-test-length scores.

standard deviation (s or σ). A measure of variability preferred over all others because of its soundness mathematically and its general usefulness as a basis for: (a) standard scores, (b) standard errors, and (c) various statistical tests of significance.

standard error. An estimate of what the *standard deviation* of a statistic would be if successive values were found for that statistic through repeated testings (usually on different, but similar, samples drawn from the same population).

standard error of estimate. A *standard deviation* based on differences between obtained scores and scores predicted (from knowledge of correlation between a predictor variable and a criterion variable), rather than differences between scores and the mean.

standard error of measurement. An estimate of the *standard deviation* that would be found in the distribution of scores for a specified person if he were to be tested again and again on the same or a similar test (assuming no learning).

standard score. Any of several derived scores (Type II A) based on number of standard deviations between a specified raw score and the mean of the distribution. See also *normalized standard score.*

standardization. The act or process of developing a *standardized test;*

many stages are involved in careful standardization, among these: tryout of items, item analyses, validation studies, reliability studies, development of norms, and the like.

standardized test. An empirically developed test, designed for administration and scoring according to stated directions, for which there is evidence of validity and reliability, as well as norms.

stanine. A *normalized standard score* (Type II B 4 b) of nine units, 1-9; in a normal distribution, stanines have a mean of 5.0 and a standard deviation of 1.96.

sten. A *normalized standard score* (Type II B 4 d), similar to the more common *stanine*, but having five units on either side of the mean; the mean sten (in a normal distribution) is 5.5, and the standard deviation is about 2.0.

stencil key. A *scoring key* made for placing over the answer sheet, the examinee's responses being visible either through holes prepared for that purpose or through the transparent material of the key itself; the IBM Test Scoring Machine uses a scoring key of this type.

strip key. A *scoring key* prepared in a column or strip which may be laid alongside a column of answers on the examinee's answer sheet or test paper; when several columns of answers are printed on the same scoring key, it becomes a "fan" or "accordion key."

subjective test. A test on which the personal opinion or impression of the scorer is one determinant of the obtained score; i.e., the scoring key cannot be (or is not) prescribed in advance of scoring.

survey test. A test designed to measure achievement in one or more specified areas, usually with the intention of assessing group understanding of the concepts, principles, and facts—rather than individual measurement.

***T*-scaled score.** A *normalized standard score* (Type II B 4 a) with a mean of 50 and a standard deviation of 10.

***T*-score.** A *standard score* (Type II A 2) which has a mean of 50 and a standard deviation of 10.

temporal reliability. Test stability over a period of time, estimated through a test-retest *reliability coefficient;* i.e., a coefficient of correlation based on scores made on the same test at two different times.

true score. A theoretical concept never obtainable in practice, an error-free score; usually defined as the average of the scores that would be obtained if a specified examinee were to take the same test an infinite number of times (assuming no learning).

truncated. Term used to describe a distribution of scores that is cut off artificially or arbitrarily at some point, whatever the reason; e.g., a distribution of test scores in which many examinees receive the maximum possible score, thereby not enabling these examinees to score as high as they could have if the test had a suitable ceiling.

typical-performance test. Any test designed to measure what an examinee is "really like," rather than any intellective or ability characteristic; category includes tests of personality, attitude, interest, etc.; used in opposition to *maximum-performance test.*

universe. See *population.*

validity. The extent to which a test does the job desired of it; the evidence may be either empirical or logical. Unless otherwise noted, *empirical validity* is implied.

variable. (1) Any trait or characteristic which may change with the individual or the observation. (2) More strictly, any representation of such a trait or characteristic which is capable of assuming different values; e.g., a test is a variable.

variable error. Any deviation from a *true score* attributable to one or more nonconstant influences, such as guessing, irregular testing conditions, etc.; always has a direct adverse effect on reliability; by definition, *variable errors* are uncorrelated with *true scores.*

work-sample test. A test on which the examinee's response to a simulated on-the-job problem or situation is evaluated; e.g., a pre-employment typing test.

DIRECTIONS FOR USING TABLE 9

Table 9 may be used to convert from one derived-score system to another, assuming a normal distribution. Simply enter the table with the score in which you are interested; all entries on the same line are its normal-curve equivalents. Care must be taken when using the table to compare results from different tests, for different norms groups are likely to be involved.

See last page of table for an explanation of symbols.

To use Table 9 for types of score *not* shown here, follow these steps:

For a linear standard score (Type II A):

1. Find the amount by which an examinee's raw score differs from the mean of the group with which you wish to compare him (either from the manual or from the local testing); i.e., $X - \bar{X}$.
2. Obtain the examinee's z-score by dividing this difference by the standard deviation of the same group; i.e., $(X - \bar{X})/s$.
3. Enter this value of z in the first column; all other entries on the same line are linear standard score equivalents (except for the percentile rank in the final column).

For a normalized standard score (Type II B 4):

1. Follow the directions for computing a percentile rank (*see* Chart 3 on pages 108-109).
2. Enter this value of percentile rank in the extreme-right-hand column of the table. All other entries on the same line of the table are now *normalized* standard-score equivalents.

. . . .

Customarily, none of these scores (except z) is expressed with a decimal. As a final step, therefore, you will usually round your score to the nearest whole number (if necessary).

TABLE 9

CONVERSION TABLE FOR DERIVED SCORES *

z $\left(\dfrac{X-\overline{X}}{s}\right)$ [Type II A1]ᵃ	Tᵇ (10z+50) [Type II A2 or II B4a]ᵃ	AGCT (20z+100) [Type II A3]ᵃ	CEEB (100z+500) [Type II A4]ᵃ	IQ Wechsler (15z+100) [Type II A5a]ᵃ	IQ Stanford-Binet (16z+100) [Type II A5b]ᵃ	Sᶜ T A N I N E [Type II B4b]ᵃ	C-Score [Type II B4c]ᵃ	Stenᶜ [Type II B4d]ᵃ	Percentile Rank [Type II B2]ᵃ
-3.00	20.	40	200	55	52				0.1
-2.95	20.5	41	205	56	53				0.2
-2.90	21.	42	210	57	54				0.2
-2.85	21.5	43	215	57	54				0.2
-2.80	22.	44	220	58	55				0.3
-2.75	22.5	45	225	59	56				0.3
-2.70	23.	46	230	60	57		0		0.4
-2.65	23.5	47	235	60	58				0.4
-2.60	24.	48	240	61	58				0.5
-2.55	24.5	49	245	62	59	1			0.5
-2.50	25.	50	250	63	60			1	0.6
-2.45	25.5	51	255	63	61				0.7
-2.40	26.	52	260	64	62				0.8
-2.35	26.5	53	265	65	62				0.9

*See directions for use on previous page.

ᵃRefers to the classification of scores developed for this book; see *Chapter VI.*

ᵇSince this table assumes a normal distribution, these values of *T* may be either T-scores (Type II A2) or T-scaled scores (Type II B4a); if the distribution were *not* normal, *T-scaled score* entries would differ.

ᶜThis score takes only a very limited number of different values; therefore, it will have the same value for a range of values on other scores.

IQ spans the Wechsler and Stanford-Binet columns.

z $\left(\frac{X-\overline{X}}{s}\right)$ [Type II A1]a	T[b] (10z+50) [Type II A2 or II B4a]a	AGCT (20z+100) [Type II A3]a	CEEB (100z+500) [Type II A4]a	Wechsler (15z+100) [Type II A5a]a	Stanford-Binet (16z+100) [Type II A5b]a	S[c] T A N I N E [Type II B4b]a	C-Score[c] [Type II B4c]a	Sten[c] [Type II B4d]a	Percentile Rank [Type II B2]a
-2.30	27	54	270	66	63		0		1.1
-2.25	27.5	55	275	66	64			1	1.2
-2.20	28.	56	280	67	65				1.4
-2.15	28.5	57	285	68	66				1.6
-2.10	29.	58	290	69	66				1.8
-2.05	29.5	59	295	69	67				2.0
-2.00	30.	60	300	70	68	1	1		2.3
-1.95	30.5	61	305	71	69				2.6
-1.90	31.	62	310	72	70				2.9
-1.85	31.5	63	315	72	70				3.2
-1.80	32.	64	320	73	71			2	3.6
-1.75	32.5	65	325	74	72				4.0
-1.70	33.	66	330	75	73				4.5
-1.65	33.5	67	335	75	74				5.0
-1.60	34.	68	340	76	74				5.5
-1.55	34.5	69	345	77	75				6.1
-1.50	35.	70	350	78	76	2	2		6.7
-1.45	35.5	71	355	78	77				7.4
-1.40	36.	72	360	79	78			3	8.1
-1.35	36.5	73	365	80	78				8.8
-1.30	37.	74	370	81	79				9.7

z $\left(\frac{X-\overline{X}}{s}\right)$ [Type II A1][a]	T^b (10z+50) [Type II A2 or II B4a][a]	AGCT (20z+100) [Type II A3][a]	CEEB (100z+500) [Type II A4][a]	IQ Wechsler (15z+100) [Type II A5a][a]	IQ Stanford-Binet (16z+100) [Type II A5b][a]	S^c T A N I N E [Type II B4b][a]	C-Score[c] [Type II B4c][a]	Sten[c] [Type II B4d][a]	Percentile Rank [Type II B2][a]
-1.25	37.5	75	375	81	80				10.6
-1.20	38.	76	380	82	81			3	11.5
-1.15	38.5	77	385	83	82				12.5
-1.10	39.	78	390	84	82				13.6
-1.05	39.5	79	395	84	83		3		14.7
-1.00	40.	80	400	85	84				15.9
-.95	40.5	81	405	86	85	3			17.1
-.90	41.	82	410	87	86				18.4
-.85	41.5	83	415	87	86				19.8
-.80	42.	84	420	88	87			4	21.2
-.75	42.5	85	425	89	88				22.7
-.70	43.	86	430	90	89		4		24.2
-.65	43.5	87	435	90	90				25.8
-.60	44.	88	440	91	90	4			27.4
-.55	44.5	89	445	92	91				29.1
-.50	45.	90	450	93	92				30.8
-.45	45.5	91	455	93	93			5	32.6
-.40	46.	92	460	94	94				34.5
-.35	46.5	93	465	95	94				36.3
-.30	47.	94	470	96	95				38.2
-.25	47.5	95	475	96	96				40.1

IQ conversion table

z $\left(\dfrac{X-\overline{X}}{s}\right)$ [Type II A1][a]	T[b] (10z + 50) [Type II A2 or II B4a][a]	AGCT (20z + 100) [Type II A3][a]	CEEB (100z + 500) [Type II A4][a]	Wechsler (15z + 100) [Type II A5a][a]	Stanford-Binet (16z + 100) [Type II A5b][a]	S[c] T A N I N E [Type II B4b][a]	C-Score[c] [Type II B4c][a]	Sten[c] [Type II B4d][a]	Percentile Rank [Type II B2][a]
− .20	48.	96	480	97	97				42.1
− .15	48.5	97	485	98	98				44.0
− .10	49.	98	490	98	98				46.0
− .05	49.5	99	495	99	99				48.0
0.00	50.	100	500	100	100	5	5	5	50.0
.05	50.5	101	505	101	101				52.0
.10	51.	102	510	102	102				54.0
.15	51.5	103	515	102	102				56.0
.20	52.	104	520	103	103				57.9
.25	52.5	105	525	104	104				59.9
.30	53.	106	530	104	105	6	6	6	61.8
.35	53.5	107	535	105	106				63.7
.40	54.	108	540	106	106				65.5
.45	54.5	109	545	107	107				67.4
.50	55.	110	550	108	108				69.2
.55	55.5	111	555	108	109				70.9
.60	56.	112	560	109	110	7	7	7	72.6
.65	56.5	113	565	110	110				74.2
.70	57.	114	570	111	111				75.8
.75	57.5	115	575	111	112				77.3
.80	58.	116	580	112	113				78.8

210

IQ

z $\left(\dfrac{X-\bar{X}}{s}\right)$ [Type II A1][a]	T[b] (10z+50) [Type II A2 or II B4a][a]	AGCT (20z+100) [Type II A3][a]	CEEB (100z+500) [Type II A4][a]	Wechsler (15z+100) [Type II A5a][a]	Stanford-Binet (16z+100) [Type II A5b][a]	STANINE[c] [Type II B4b][a]	C-Score[c] [Type II B4c][a]	Sten[c] [Type II B4d][a]	Percentile Rank [Type II B2][a]
.85	58.5	117	585	113	114				80.2
.90	59.	118	590	114	114	7		7	81.6
.95	59.5	119	595	114	115		7		82.9
1.00	60.	120	600	115	116				84.1
1.05	60.5	121	605	116	117				85.3
1.10	61.	122	610	117	118				86.4
1.15	61.5	123	615	117	118				87.5
1.20	62.	124	620	118	119				88.5
1.25	62.5	125	625	119	120			8	89.4
1.30	63.	126	630	120	121	8			90.3
1.35	63.5	127	635	120	122		8		91.2
1.40	64.	128	640	121	122				91.9
1.45	64.5	129	645	122	123				92.6
1.50	65.	130	650	123	124				93.3
1.55	65.5	131	655	123	125				93.9
1.60	66.	132	660	124	126			9	94.5
1.65	66.5	133	665	125	126		9		95.0
1.70	67.	134	670	126	127	9			95.5
1.75	67.5	135	675	126	128				96.0
1.80	68.	136	680	127	129				96.4
1.85	68.5	137	685	128	130				96.8

$\frac{X-\bar{X}}{s}$ [Type II A1][a]	T[b] (10z+50) [Type II A2 or II B4a][a]	AGCT (20z+100) [Type II A3][a]	CEEB (100z+500) [Type II A4][a]	IQ Wechsler (15z+100) [Type II A5a][a]	IQ Stanford-Binet (16z+100) [Type II A5b][a]	S[c] TANINE [Type II B4b][a]	C-Score[c] [Type II B4c][a]	Sten[c] [Type II B4d][a]	Percentile Rank [Type II B2][a]
1.90	69.	138	690	129	130				97.1
1.95	69.5	139	695	129	131			9	97.4
2.00	70.	140	700	130	132				97.7
2.05	70.5	141	705	131	133		9		98.0
2.10	71.	142	710	132	134	9			98.2
2.15	71.5	143	715	132	134				98.4
2.20	72.	144	720	133	135				98.6
2.25	72.5	145	725	134	136				98.8
2.30	73.	146	730	135	137				98.9
2.35	73.5	147	735	135	138			10	99.1
2.40	74.	148	740	136	138				99.2
2.45	74.5	149	745	137	139				99.3
2.50	75.	150	750	138	140		10		99.4
2.55	75.5	151	755	138	141				99.5
2.60	76.	152	760	139	142				99.5
2.65	76.5	153	765	140	142				99.6
2.70	77.	154	770	141	143				99.6
2.75	77.5	155	775	141	144				99.7
2.80	78.	156	780	142	145				99.7
2.85	78.5	157	785	143	146				99.8
2.90	79.	158	790	144	146				99.8
2.95	79.5	159	795	144	147				99.8
3.00	80.	160	800	145	148				99.9

TABLE 10

SUMMARY OF SCORE CHARACTERISTICS

Symbols explained on page 223
All scores explained in more detail in *Chapter VI*

Type I: based on absolute standard; or content difficulty

Classification Type	Name, Symbol, & Formula	Rationale	Advantages	Limitations	In a normal distribution, the derived-score value at these three selected points will be:		
					at $\overline{X}$	1s below $\overline{X}$	2s above $\overline{X}$
I A	Percentage Correct $X_{\%c} = 100 \ R/T$	States score as a percentage of maximum possible score.	1. Widely used with informal tests. 2. Doesn't depend on scores of other E's.	1. Not suited for use with standardized tests. 2. $\overline{X}$ and s differ for every test and group. 3. Doesn't express E's score relative to other E's.	*cannot say*		
I B	Letter Grade (sometimes)	Expresses E's score according to arbitrary quality standard.	1. Widely used, especially in schools and colleges. 2. Doesn't depend on scores of other E's.	1. Not suited for use with standardized tests. 2. Each test and group yields unique distribution. 3. Doesn't express E's score relative to other E's.	*cannot say*		

Symbols explained on page 223
All scores explained in more detail in *Chapter VI*

Type II: Based on Interindividual Comparisons
II A: Considering Mean and Standard Deviation (linear standard scores)

Classification Type	Name, Symbol, & Formula	Rationale	Advantages	Limitations	In a normal distribution, the derived-score value at these three selected points will be:		
					at X̄	1s below X̄	2s above X̄
II A 1	z-score (rarely, sigma-score) $z = (X - \bar{X})/s$	Expresses score as number of s's away from X̄.	1. Gives common X̄ (0.00) and s (1.00) to every test and group. 2. Distribution of z-scores is exact same shape as for raw scores on which they're based. 3. Normal probability table entries are stated as z-scores. 4. Many advantages for research, including: basis for other linear standard scores, standard errors, etc.	1. About half of scores have minus signs. 2. Score units are too coarse unless shown to 1 or 2 decimal places.	0	-1.00	+2.00

214

Symbols explained on page 223
All scores explained in more detail in *Chapter VI*

Classification Type	Name, Symbol, & Formula	Rationale	Advantages	Limitations	In a normal distribution, the derived-score value at these three selected points will be:		
					at $\bar{X}$	1s below $\bar{X}$	2s above $\bar{X}$
II A 2	T-score T = 10z + 50	Same as for z-score, except that $\bar{X}$ = 50 and s = 10.	Avoids limitations of z-score thru use of multiplying constant (10) and additive constant (50).	1. Meaning less obvious than z. 2. Less useful statistically than z. 3. Values easily confused with PR's and other scores using same numbers.	50	40	70
II A 3	AGCT-score AGCT = 20z + 100	Same as for z-score, except that $\bar{X}$ = 100 and s = 20; developed for *Army General Classification Test* during World War II.	Avoids limitations of z-score thru use of multiplying constant (20) and additive constant (100).	1 & 2. Same as above. 3. Values easily confused with IQ's and other scores using same numbers.	100	80	140

215

Symbols explained on page 223
All scores explained in more detail in *Chapter VI*

Classification Type	Name, Symbol, & Formula	Rationale	Advantages	Limitations	In a normal distribution, the derived-score value at these three selected points will be:		
					at $\bar{X}$	1s below $\bar{X}$	2s above $\bar{X}$
II A 4	CEEB-score $CEEB = 100z + 500$	Same as for z-score, except that $\bar{X} = 500$ and s = 100; developed by Educational Testing Service for use with College Board and other examinations.	Avoids limitations of z-score thru use of multiplying constant (100) and additive constant (500).	1 & 2. Same as above. 3. Large range may encourage over-interpretation of score differences.	500	400	700
II A 5 a	Deviation IQ: Wechsler $IQ_{Wechsler} = 15z + 100$	Approximates values of ratio IQ (Type III A), but makes s constant (15) at all ages; developed for use with Wechsler intelligence tests.	1. Similar to z-score. 2. Makes IQ's more comparable from age to age.	1. IQ's less well-understood than generally assumed. 2. May be confused with other scores using same numbers.	100	85	130

216

Symbols explained on page 223
All scores explained in more detail in *Chapter VI*

Classification Type	Name, Symbol, & Formula	Rationale	Advantages	Limitations	In a normal distribution, the derived-score value at these three selected points will be:		
					at $\overline{X}$	1s below $\overline{X}$	2s above $\overline{X}$
II A 5 b	Deviation IQ: Stanford-Binet $IQ_{SB} = 16z + 100$	Approximates values of ratio IQ (Type III A), but makes s constant (16) for all ages; developed for use with the *Stanford-Binet Intelligence Scale.*	1 & 2. Same as above.	1 & 2. Same as above.	100	84	132
II B: Considering Rank Within Stated Group							
II B 1	Rank	Expresses score simply as rank within stated group.	Easily understood	Completely dependent on N in group.	*cannot say*		
II B 2	Percentile Rank PR	Based on cf; states percentage of E's at or below given raw-score value.	1. Widely used and easily understood. 2. Probably best all-around type of derived score, especially with percentile band modification.	1. Units not equal in size; values overemphasize differences near median. 2. Overemphasizes differences when test is short. 3. Has limited use in research.	50	16	98

Symbols explained on page 223
All scores explained in more detail in *Chapter VI*

Classification Type	Name Symbol, & Formula	Rationale	Advantages	Limitations	In a normal distribution, the derived-score value at these three selected points will be:		
					at X̄	1s below X̄	2s above X̄
II B 3	Letter Grade (sometimes)	Expresses performance relative to other E's in group.	Considers relative performance (Type I B does not).	Takes only limited number of values (usually: A, B, C, D, and F).	*cannot say*		
II B 4: Normalized Standard Scores							
II B 4 a	T-scaled score	Similar to T-score (Type II A2), but found through cf's.	Makes distribution more nearly normal.	1. Less valuable for research than *linear* standard scores (II A). 2. Easily confused with other scores using same numbers. 3. Changes shape of original distribution.	50	40	70
II B 4 b	Stanine	9-unit scale; each unit (except extremes, 1 & 9) is 1/2-s wide in normal distribution.	1. Gives maximum information for 9-unit scale. 2. Reasonably easy to understand; becoming more popular.	1. Not widely used (yet) or understood. 2. Takes only 9 different values.	5	3	9

Symbols explained on page 223

All scores explained in more detail in *Chapter VI*

Classification Type	Name, Symbol, & Formula	Rationale	Advantages	Limitations	In a normal distribution, the derived-score value at these three selected points will be:		
					at $\bar{X}$	1s below $\bar{X}$	2s above $\bar{X}$
II B 4 c	C-score	Same as stanine (above), but has one more unit at each extreme.	Similar to stanine (above).	Similar to stanine (above).	5	3	9
II B 4 d	Sten	Same as stanine (above), but has 10 units--5 on either side of $\bar{X}$.	Similar to stanine (above).	Similar to stanine (above).	5-6	3-4	9-10
II B 4 e	Deviation IQ (sometimes)	Similar to T-scaled score (above), but with $\bar{X} = 100$ to resemble ratio IQ (Type III A).	1. Controls size of s to some extent. 2. Has more normal distribution than raw scores.	1. Not widely used. 2. Usual limitations of deviation IQ's.	100	*depends on test author*	
II B 4 f	ITED-score	Similar to T-scaled score (above), but with different $\bar{X}$ and s.	Has more normal distribution than raw scores.	Not widely used.	15	10	25

Symbols explained on page 223
All scores explained in more detail in *Chapter VI*

Classification Type	Name, Symbol, & Formula	Rationale	Advantages	Limitations	In a normal distribution, the derived-score value at these three selected points will be:		
					at $\overline{X}$	1s below $\overline{X}$	2s above $\overline{X}$
II B 5	Decile Rank DR (rare)	Similar to percentile rank (Type II B2); based on cf's; expressed as nearest decile point.	Avoids overemphasis of differences in short test (see Limitation #2, Percentile Rank).	1. Overemphasizes small differences near median. 2. Can take only 11 different values.	5	2	10
II C: Considering the Range of Scores in a Group							
II C 1	Per Cent Placement $X_{\%p1} = 100 \times (X - L)/(H - L)$	Expresses E's score as percentage of distance between highest and lowest scores made.	An interesting modification of a percentage correct score.	1. Depends completely on two extreme scores. 2. Used rarely-and never with standardized tests.	*cannot say*		
II D: Considering Status of Those Obtaining Same Score							
II D 1	Age Scores (II D1a, Mental Age; II D1b, Educational Ages)	Expresses E's score as the age of those for whom the same raw score is the average.	1. Apparently easy to understand, especially at younger ages. 2. Provides basis for Type III scores.	1. Less obvious in meaning than they seem. 2. s varies with group and with test.	*cannot say*		

Symbols explained on page 223
All scores explained in more detail in *Chapter VI*

Classification Type	Name, Symbol, & Formula	Rationale	Advantages	Limitations	In a normal distribution, the derived-score value at these three selected points will be:		
					at $\overline{X}$	1s below $\overline{X}$	2s above $\overline{X}$
II D 2	Grade-Placement Scores (see *Chapter VI* for sub-types)	Expresses E's score as the grade-placement of pupils for whom E's raw score is the average.	1. Reasonably sound "inherent" meaning for lower grades. 2. Uses units which are familiar to school teachers (i.e., grade-equivalents).	1. Less meaningful than it seems. 2. Values easy to confuse with standards that "should be" attained. 3. Size of s varies widely from one subject-matter to another, especially at higher grades'. 4. Almost impossible to compare E's performance from one test to another.	*cannot say*		

Symbols explained on page 223
All scores explained in more detail in *Chapter VI*

III: Intraindividual Comparison (of Two Measures of Individual)

Classification Type	Name, Symbol, & Formula	Rationale	Advantages	Limitations	In a normal distribution, the derived-score value at these three selected points will be:		
					at $\overline{X}$	1s below $\overline{X}$	2s above $\overline{X}$
III A	Ratio IQ (Intelligence Quotient) IQ = 100 MA/CA	An index of brightness found by comparing E's MA (from intelligence test) with his CA; the original notion of "IQ."	1. Reasonably sound "inherent" meaning among children. 2. General concept widely understood (but only incompletely).	1. Not understood thoroughly by many test users. 2. s varies widely with test and from age to age within same test. 3. Less commonly used today than formerly.	100	*cannot say*	
III B	Intellectual Status Index	Similar to ratio IQ (above) except that the average CA (for E's grade placement) is substituted for E's CA.	E's *measured* intelligence *may* be determined more by his years of schooling than by his actual CA.	1. Similar to ratio IQ (above). 2. Used by only one publisher (California Test Bureau)	100	*cannot say*	

Symbols explained below)
All scores explained in more detail in *Chapter VI*

Classification Type	Name, Symbol, & Formula	Rationale	Advantages	Limitations	In a normal distribution, the derived-score value at these three selected points will be:		
					at $\overline{X}$	1s below $\overline{X}$	2s above $\overline{X}$
III C	Educational Quotient EQ = 100 EA/CA	Expresses E's performance on achievement test as ratio of EA to CA.	(If any) similar to ratio IQ (above).	s varies so much with test and with age that few generalizations can be made.		*cannot say*	
III D	Accomplishment Quotient AQ = 100 EA/MA	Presumes to measure ratio of achievement to intelligence.	None.	Most erroneous type of score (*see Chapter VI*)			

IV: Assorted Arbitrary Bases (See Chapter VI)

SYMBOLS USED IN THIS TABLE:

CA   Chronological age.
cf   Cumulative frequency; i.e., the sum of frequencies up through a given score value.
E   Examinee.
EA   Educational ages (score Type II D1b).
H   Highest score made.
IQ   Intelligence quotient.
L   Lowest score made.
MA   Mental age.

N   Number of examinees in a specified group.
PR   Percentile rank.
R   Number of right answers (on a test paper).
s   Standard deviation.
T   Total number of items on a test.
W   Number of wrong answers (on a test paper).
X   Raw score on a test.
$\overline{X}$ Mean raw score for a specified group of examinees.
z   z-score.